YOUNG BOSWELL

James Boswell.

YOUNG BOSWELL

CHAPTERS ON
JAMES BOSWELL THE BIOGRAPHER
BASED LARGELY ON NEW MATERIAL

By

CHAUNCEY BREWSTER TINKER

With Many Illustrations

THE ATLANTIC MONTHLY PRESS
BOSTON

To R. B. ADAM

My dear Mr. Adam,

Since it was our common interest in Boswell that brought us acquainted now many years ago, you will, I am sure, permit me to dedicate this book to you. You have furnished me with a large number of the new letters which are quoted in it, and with nearly all the illustrations. But I value even more highly your unfailing interest in me and in my studies. In more senses than one this book is already your own.

Faithfully yours,

Chauncey B. Tinker.

PREFACE

To write the life of him who was himself the Great Biographer is a task which I have had no thought of attempting in this book.   In the course of collecting the letters of Boswell I have come across a good many new incidents in his career, which, it has seemed to me, might perhaps alter, or at least ameliorate, the view generally held of him, and which might properly be made the subject of a group of connected essays.   In each essay there is, I think, a good deal of new information, for the sources of which I refer the reader to my forthcoming edition of Boswell's correspondence. But though a large part of my material is new, I have not hesitated to draw also upon older and more familiar matter.   The quotations from Boswell's letters to Temple are from the original manuscript, now in the possession of Mr. John Pierpont Morgan, which has not been studied since 1857.   I take this opportunity of thanking Mr. Morgan for permitting me to copy it.   In using extracts from it I have retained, as elsewhere, Boswell's spelling, but not his punctuation.

To my friend Dr. J. T. T. Brown of Glasgow, who has been a lifelong student of Boswell and who has taken a keen interest in my labours from

PREFACE

their inception, I offer my warmest thanks. Mr. Clement Shorter has kindly permitted me to reprint in Chapter IX a portion of the essay that I contributed to the ninth volume of his edition of Boswell's *Johnson*, as an introduction to the *Journal of a Tour to the Hebrides*.

In one way, perhaps, this book may be unique. James Boswell has fared rather badly at the hands of most people who have written about him. For myself, I frankly admit that I have enjoyed my association with him, and that I have had no desire either to patronise him or to sit in judgment on his occasional lapses from social propriety and moral standards. That Boswell was at times a very foolish young man any reader may see; but he was not, I think, so foolish as many of his critics have been. When all is said, he had genius, and of that I have tried to make a sympathetic study, preferring to err, if I must err, on the side of appreciation.

C. B. T.

Yale University
February 23, 1922.

CONTENTS

ILLUSTRATIONS

ILLUSTRATIONS

CHRONOLOGY

1740. Born, October 29, at Edinburgh.

1758. Earliest specimens of his correspondence with William Temple.

1759. Enters class in Moral Philosophy under Adam Smith at Glasgow University.

1760. First Visit to London.

1761. Returns to Edinburgh.
Publishes an "Ode to Tragedy."

1763. Second Visit to London.
Publishes his correspondence with Andrew Erskine.
Meets Samuel Johnson "in the back shop of Mr. Thomas Davies, the bookseller, in Russell Street, Covent Garden," May 16.
Studies law at Utrecht.

1764. At Berlin.
Visits Geneva.
Meets Rousseau at Motiers.
Meets Voltaire at Ferney.

1765. Meets Wilkes in Italy.
In Corsica. Intimacy with General Paoli.

1766. Returns to London; and then to Scotland.
Admitted to the bar in Edinburgh, July 26.

1768. Publishes "An Account of Corsica, with Memoirs of General Paoli."
Visits London.

CHRONOLOGY

1769. Publishes "British Essays in favour of the Brave Corsicans," by several hands.

Marries his cousin, Margaret Montgomery of Lainshaw.

1773. Elected to Literary Club, April 30.

Visits the Hebrides with Dr. Johnson, August 18–November 22.

1782. Succeeds to his father's estate.

1784. Death of Samuel Johnson.

1785. Publishes "A Journal of the Tour to the Hebrides."

1785. Takes up his residence in London.

1786. Called to the English bar.

1790. Defeated for Parliament.

1791. Publishes the "Life of Johnson," May 16.

1793. Publishes the second edition of the "Life of Johnson."

1795. Dies, May 19.

YOUNG BOSWELL

YOUNG BOSWELL

CHAPTER I

YOUNG BOSWELL

You will laugh at my whim and be sorry for my weakness.
— BOSWELL to TEMPLE, 12 *July*, 1763.

ONE of the rarest books in the world is a thin
volume in quarto, called "An Ode to Tragedy,"
and described on the title-page as the work of "a
Gentleman of Scotland." It is one of the earliest
of James Boswell's fugitive works, and appeared
at Edinburgh as a sixpenny pamphlet in the year
1761, although, by an odd error in proof-reading,
the date on the title-page is 1661. The author,
who was but twenty years of age, was certainly
no poet. He aspired, he announced, to soar on
pinions bold, "and, like the skylark, at heaven's
gate to sing"; but his mechanical verses proved
to be as dull as a music-box. There is, to be sure,
a description of Garrick in the rôle of King Lear,
which one reads with a sort of interest because of
the intimacy which was later to exist between
Boswell and the actor; and there are references to
Mason and the elder Sheridan which are worth a

AN

ODE

TO

TRAGEDY.

By a GENTLEMAN of SCOTLAND.

EDINBURGH:

Printed by A. DONALDSON and J. REID.

For ALEX. DONALDSON.

MDCLXI.

[Price SIX PENCE.]

glance; but it is not in such allusions that the value
of the book consists. The remarkable thing about
it is its Dedication. It is inscribed to James Boswell, Esq. The author, with a humour worthy of a
more famous publication, has genially dedicated
the book to himself.

But, one asks, was the reader supposed to discover the jest? Boswell, I fancy, did not greatly
care, one way or the other. He had given the
reader a hint that he was up to mischief, for he
wrote in the dedicatory letter: "I make no doubt,
Sir, but you consider me as your very good friend;
although some people — and those, too, not desti-
tute of wisdom — will not scruple to insinuate
the contrary." If the reader were sharp-witted
enough to detect the imposture, he would certainly spread the news of his discovery, and with
it the fame of the young author. But if he missed
the point, Boswell would be no loser, for he would
then be regarded as the poet's patron. In either
case, it might be hoped, people would talk about
James Boswell. Perhaps, on the whole, he preferred the reputation of patron to that of poet, for
he was ever ambitious to be deemed a Mæcenas
— a sufficiently rare ambition in a youth of twenty
summers. Indeed, he had already appeared in this
rôle. His friend, Francis Gentleman, an actor of
Glasgow, had published an edition of the well-known

tragedy of "Oroonoco" in the previous year, and
had dedicated it to Boswell; the young man has
been suspected, not without reason, of having written the dedicatory verses himself. Moreover, when,
a few years later, his friend Derrick (Beau Nash's
successor as Master of Ceremonies at Bath) published a series of letters descriptive of Ireland and
of the English Lakes, Boswell persuaded him to
address one of them to "James Boswell, Esq., of
Authenleck [so Derrick misprinted the name],
North-Britain." It is clear that Boswell's ambition
was peculiar. He desired to be known as the associate of authors. The glory, to his way of thinking,
is to move in the world of literary men, to know
what is going on, and in time, perhaps, to become
an influence in the lives of these great ones. It was
his ambition to shine, but he preferred to shine in
a reflected light.   Many years after, a relative remarked, "He preferred being a showman to keeping a shop of his own."

This ruling passion of Boswell's — the passion
not to occupy the throne, or even to be the power
behind it, but to stand near the throne as the
monarch's acknowledged friend — is a sufficiently
unusual phenomenon, and harshly has it been
judged.   It would be interesting to speculate why
Boswell's desire to associate with men of genius
should have moved the critics to violent indig-

nation. It is surely a little odd that a man who has provided the world with two of the most delightful, profitable, and amusing books of all time should have been denounced as a toad-eater and a lick-spittle. One would think that the means by which he developed his innate genius might have been studied with seriousness, if not with sympathy, and that what most critics have been content to call an appetite for notoriety might have been discovered by the discriminating to be, in truth, a commendable ambition. But the fact is that few critics have been fitted to understand, much less to interpret, Boswell's curious sense of humour. He was a man who not only enjoyed a joke, but enjoyed it the more when it was directed at himself. He was not unwilling to be the butt, provided only that there might be wit and hilarity. In the year following the appearance of his "Ode to Tragedy," he published another poem, celebrating his social exploits in London, entitled "The Cub at Newmarket," and dedicated to the Duke of York. "Permit me to let the world know," he remarked in the Dedication, "that the same cub has been laughed at by the Duke of York." Boswell was, and ever remained, willing to sacrifice himself that the company might laugh.

And now, O reader, if all this disgusts or pains you, pray close the book and read in it no more,

for the story of James Boswell is not for you.
There are serious and admirable books for those
who wish to associate with an author who is consistently modest and dignified, and who, if he
indulges in humour, never forgets to maintain a
certain propriety, lest the reader call him a fool.
But the story of James Boswell is for those who
are ready and able to realise that greatness may be
linked with folly or, indeed, spring out of it.

If, then, association with the Great on terms of
easy intimacy was the ambition of his youth, it
was no more than he had a right to feel that he
might achieve. He was no social upstart. Nothing could be further from the truth than to conceive of him as coming out of some vague middle
class, with a cheap desire to raise himself by
catching at the skirts of the eminent. If it were
permissible to employ the standards of fine society,
it would not be unfair to say that in the association
with Johnson it was Boswell who conferred upon
the older man the social distinction. A descendant
of Robert the Bruce, with the blood of half a
dozen earls flowing in his veins, might, it is to be
hoped, be pardoned for aspiring to associate with
the son of a country bookseller! There was, of
course, a difference in age, nationality, and achievement that must be reckoned with; but, allowing
for all this, there was no reason why young Boswell

should hesitate to claim his right to enter the most distinguished society of the realm.

His father, Alexander Boswell of Auchinleck, was one of the most prominent members of the landed gentry of Southern Scotland, and an advocate of high distinction. Upon his elevation to the judicial bench, he had assumed, according to Scottish custom, the title of Lord Auchinleck.[1] His estate at Auchinleck, in Ayrshire, had been conferred upon his ancestor, Thomas Boswell, by royal grant in 1504. This founder of a long line had been killed in battle at Flodden Field, together with the sovereign who had been his benefactor. Nor was Boswell's descent less distinguished on his mother's side. She was Euphemia Erskine, through whom he might claim kinship with the Earls of Mar and Dundonald. Finally, as he proudly relates, from his great grandfather, Alexander, Earl of Kincardine, the blood of Bruce flowed in his veins.

The estate of the family had been judiciously increased until, in the days of Boswell, the laird of Auchinleck could ride ten miles forward from the door of his house without leaving his own land; upon this vast tract were no less than six

[1] This title, however, like episcopal titles in England, could not be inherited; neither did it confer upon the holder's wife the privileges of a peeress. Thus Lord Auchinleck's wife remained "Mrs. Boswell."

hundred people, attached to him as overlord.
Here Boswell's father had erected a palace declared
(upon somewhat doubtful local testimony) to be
the work of the Adam brothers, and a worthy centre
to the family seat which it dominated. Above
the Romanesque portal, in an elaborately carved
tympanum, is the Boswellian crest—a hooded fal-
con proper—and other
allegorical symbols.

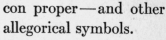

Through the grounds
flow the river Lugar
and a stream called the
Dipple, which empties
into it. There are deep
chasms, steep descents to the water, and romantic
cliffs. On the banks of the Lugar are the ruins
of the original castle, and between these and
the house, the remains of a former mansion.
Boswell told Johnson that in youth he had
"appropriated the finest descriptions in the ancient classics" to certain scenes on his ancestral
estates. Years later, when Johnson visited the
place, after the tour to the Hebrides, he
wrote: "Lord Auchinleck has built a house of
hewn stone, very stately and durable, and has
advanced the value of his lands, with great ten-
derness to his tenants. I was, however, less delighted with the elegance of the modern mansion,

Ruins of the Old Castle, Auchinleck

" I was," said Dr. Johnson, " less delighted with the elegance of the modern mansion than with the sullen dignity of the old castle."

than with the sullen dignity of the old castle." It
was of this castle that he had said, when Boswell
first described it to him, "I must be there, Sir,
and we will live in the old castle; and if there is
not a room in it remaining, we will build one."

And yet all this was not enough to satisfy the
young fellow who was heir apparent to it all. It
was inconveniently distant from cities and the
haunts of men. His father had, to be sure, a
house in Edinburgh. In Edinburgh James had
been born; there he had gone to school; there for
a time he had attended the university. But he
longed for the true centre of culture and of social
life, and that, he knew, was London. His father
knew everybody in Scotland. There was no one
there whom he, too, might not know. But the
air of provinciality galled him, even in Edinburgh.
In Auchinleck it was intolerable.

Over the main portal of the house at Auchinleck Boswell's father had had carved a quotation
from the Epistles of Horace, in the choice of
which, it might almost seem, he had his restless
son in mind: —

Quod petis hic est,
Est Ulubris, animus si te non deficit æquus.

Ulubrae, a town near the Pontine marshes of
Latium, had been a byword among the Latin
authors for its remoteness from Rome, and Boswell

never scrupled to admit that he had not the
animus æquus necessary to the enjoyment of a
modern Scottish Ulubrae. Even after it was his
own, he referred sarcastically to himself, when
writing to John Wilkes, as the "Master of Ulubrae," and he remained consistently unwilling to
exile himself there. Absent from London, he was
ever restless. At the age of twenty, after his first
visit to London, he spoke with transport of the
town where his thoughts of happiness had "always
centred," where he had got his mind filled with
the most "gay ideas — getting into the Guards,
being about Court, enjoying the happiness of the
beau monde, and the company of men of genius."
And at the age of fifty-four, when his days were
numbered, he wrote to his brother David from
Auchinleck : —

I am pleased to see that the meeting of Parliament is
prorogued to the twenty-fifth of November, as I shall
have three weeks more without that additional impatience which the knowledge of the town being full, and
important affairs agitated, and the Literary Club, &c.,
going on, cannot but produce. Perhaps I may weather
it out here till January. . . . How hard it is that I do
not enjoy this fine place.

But Boswell's desire for the society of the Great
was of a peculiar kind. To the titled aristocracy
and to the merely wealthy he was, on the whole,

indifferent, unless they had something other to offer than rank or riches. At one time in his life, for example, he was privileged to meet and converse with King George III; but the honour seems to have made slight impression on him, compared with his association with men of genius; for he makes but the vaguest reference to it in his works. It was literary genius that he desired to find.

Boswell first comes before us at the age of seventeen years and nine months; his biography before that is a mere skeleton of dates and anecdotes. On July 29, 1758, he wrote to his lifelong friend, William Temple, the first of his letters which has come down to us. There is much in it about the reading of history and of poetry; but the most significant passage, in the light of what Boswell was destined to become, is an account of his first meeting with David Hume. Temple had, in some way or other, been able to procure Boswell an introduction to him, and the account of the conversation is a clear indication of what Boswell sought in such intercourse. Hume, who was almost thirty years older than Boswell, had by now attained the age of forty-seven, and was engaged in completing his "History of England." In the previous year he had written his essay on the "Natural History of Religion," which had served to spread his popular reputation as an atheist.

Some days ago [writes Boswell], I was introduced to your friend Mr. Hume; he is a most discreet, affable man as ever I met with, and has realy a great deal of learning, and a choice collection of books. He is indeed an extraordinary man, few such people are to be met with nowadays. We talk a great deal of genius, fine language, improving our style, etc., but, I am afraid, sollid learning is much wore out. Mr. Hume, I think, is a very proper person for a young man to cultivate an acquaintance with; though he has not, perhaps, the most delicate taste, yet he has apply'd himself with great attention to the study of the ancients, and is likeways a great historian, so that you are not only entertained in his company, but may reap a great deal of usefull instruction. I own myself much obliged to you, dear Sir, for procuring me the pleasure of his acquaintance.

This, I submit, is rather remarkable from a youth of seventeen, writing to his chum! For Boswell, an ideal association with an older man implies "sollid learning," delicate taste, useful instruction, and an entertaining style. Any modern parent or teacher would be inclined to rest content with thus much ambition in a boy of seventeen, if, indeed, he could rid his mind of the fear that it was all a hoax. James sits in judgment upon the qualifications of David Hume, the philosopher, as calmly—and, perhaps, as discriminatingly—as his father pronounced judgment upon a poacher at the assizes. The boy detected a lack in Hume,

and it is the very one which the philosophers
and bluestockings of the Parisian salons felt in
him when he visited them five years later. Hume
had not delicacy of taste. What he lacked was ur-
banity. Madame du Deffand described him as a
gros drôle, and Madame Geoffrin called him a peas-
ant. Learning, according to our youthful critic,
though it should be "sollid" need not be leaden.[1]

All this interest in wit and instructive conversation might easily, it would seem, have made
young James into a prig. He was in a fair way to
become that most dreadful of young things, a boy
of large inexperience who fancies himself a philosopher and a man of the world. But he was in
no danger of this. His love of convivial pleasure,
which later plunged him into gulfs of misery,
saved him at least from this. He had as much
difficulty as any schoolboy ever had in sticking to
his studies; just as, later on, he found it impos-

[1] Years did not change the original impression which
Boswell formed of the conversation of David Hume. He
heard him talk often, but seldom found anything very pointed
or profound to record. Nearly thirty years later, he wrote:
"He was cheerful, obliging and instructive; he was charitable
to the poor; and many an agreeable hour have I passed with
him. I have preserved some entertaining and interesting
memoirs of him, particularly when he knew himself to be
dying, which I may, some time or other, communicate to the
world." But it is significant that there was never sufficient
interest to spur him to the fulfillment of his promise.

sible to stick to any course of reading that he might
lay out for himself. His mind was eager and
curious, rather than progressive. He resided, for
brief periods, at Edinburgh University and at
Glasgow University, but in both places his social
instincts defeated anything like an orderly education. He had, it is true, more learning, liberal
and professional, than his critics and biographers
have been willing to allow him; but his passion
for companionship kept him always on the rove.
At one time he attached himself to Sir David
Dalrymple; at another time, to a company of
actors. He knew no rest until he found his rest in
Johnson.

And who shall say that he was wrong? After
all possible perfection of systems and courses of
study and methods of instruction, liberal education remains a personal relationship. Who would
not barter the methods of all the schools for a conversation with Socrates? Boswell's relations with
Johnson, in which he found, not merely wit and
instruction, but stimulus to achievement and the
awakening of powers within himself which he had
never realised, are a vindication of that instinct
within him which drove him to seek out the
society of men of letters. To assert that Boswell
found in such society the fulfillment of the intellectual life of which he had dreamed is not to say

that every bluestocking and moonstruck young philosopher can do the same. The distinctive feature in Boswell is the capacity for realising and using the richness of the life to which he was admitted. For this, as we shall see later, he was specially qualified.

Another force which tended to keep him from priggishness was a *naïveté* the equal of which it would be difficult to discover. Pepys's was no larger, though it was more natural; Rousseau's was no larger, though it was less comic. Perhaps no better illustration of it can be given than the inscription which he himself wrote in a copy of a book called "The Government of the Tongue," — "Presented to me by my worthy freind, Bennet Langton, Esq: of Langton, as a Book by which I might be much improved, viz. by the Government of the Tongue. He gave me the Book and hoped I would read that treatise; but said no more. I have expressed in words what I beleive was his meaning. It was a delicate admonition." A naïve person, I suppose, is one who, being profoundly interested in his own personality, makes the unwarranted assumption that other people are similarly interested in it. A few sentences from an early letter to Sir David Dalrymple, regarding the approaching sojourn in Utrecht, are, it seems to me, a classical example of *naïveté:* —

James Boswell
London 1779.

Presented to me by my
worthy freind Bennet Langton
Esqr. of Langton, as a Book
by which I might be
much improved, viz
by The Government
of the Tongue. He
gave me the Book
and hoped I would
read that treatise:
but said no more.
I have expressed
in words what I
believe was his mea:
:ning. It was a deli:
:cate admonition.

My great object is to attain a proper conduct in life. How sad will it be, if I turn no better than I am. I have much vivacity, which leads me to dissipation and folly. This, I think, I can restrain. But I will be moderate, and not aim at a stiff sageness and buckram correctness. I must, however, own to you that I have at bottom a melancholy cast; which dissipation relieves by making me thoughtless, and therefore, an easier, though a more contemptible animal. I dread a return of this malady. I am always apprehensive of it. Pray tell me if Utrecht be a place of a dull and severe cast, or if it be a place of decency and chearfull politeness? Tell me, too, if years do not strengthen the mind, and make it less susceptible of being hurt? and if having a rational object will not keep up my spirits?

There are those who find in such an utterly frank revelation of what is going on in a human breast something quite captivating. They learn to laugh at it without sneering at it. So, we may imagine, did Sir David. When Madame du Deffand read the "Tour to Corsica," she declared herself (to Horace Walpole, of all people), "*extrêmement contente*"; and elsewhere, "J'aime l'auteur à la folie; son cœur est excellent, son âme est pleine de vertus; je vais être en garde à ne pas laisser voir l'engouement que j'ai de son ouvrage." The blind sibyl of the Parisian salons, who had spent her life with sophistication, knew well the value of *naïveté* — and the wisdom of concealing it.

Of the melancholy which Boswell describes to
Sir David, and which he links with his dissipation,
something must be said, if only for the reason that
Boswell himself said so much of it. He perpetually insisted that he was, at bottom, a melancholy
man. The fear of it was ever present in his mind;
it darkened his youth, and it shrouded his latter
days in misery. He described its symptoms to all
his friends, and made pathetic appeals to them to
help him get the better of it. All this, not unnaturally, bored his friends exceedingly, for friends
do not care to hear of your blues and your fore-
bodings. It may be the duty of friends to help
you bear your burden, but if you wish to retain
them, it is best to bear it yourself without help.
Perhaps Boswell's friends would have been more
indulgent if the victim's melancholy had not taken
flight immediately upon their arrival, whereupon
they kindly assumed that his woes were imaginary.
Perhaps they were. But what misery is more
dreadful than that which resides in the imagination alone? Are not the insane so afflicted?

Again, it is true that Boswell's melancholy was
of that strikingly familiar kind which descends
upon us just as we approach some period of pro-
tracted work. His spirits always revived at the
prospect of a holiday. In a word, our Boswell was
lazy. But this is not an end of the matter. If

your friend is sick, it may be that there is a remedy that will restore him to health; but so long as he does not use it, he will remain sick. It may well be that Boswell's melancholy was of a sort which afflicts the majority of men, and which the majority of men get rid of by a little dogged pluck; but the fact remains that Boswell did not get rid of his, except at moments, and we shall understand him the better if we do not belittle his suffering. Imaginary or not, it was there, and there it remained. He talked about it too much, and for that his friends have found it hard to forgive him.

The letter that follows was addressed to one of his dearest friends, but one of whom the readers of his biography know little — John Johnston of Grange. He was, as the following letter makes evident, a boyhood friend, who had become a solicitor and who had taken charge of Boswell's private affairs during his absence from Scotland. There was nothing literary about the friendship between the two, and therefore Boswell never had occasion to mention Johnston, as he did almost all his other friends, when he published the "Life of Johnson." But Johnston was apparently a quiet and affectionate person, and is mentioned in the letters several times as "worthy Grange." This is the only letter of Boswell's to him which is known to exist.

LONDON, 30 *June*, 1763.

MY DEAR FRIEND, —

I have been dissapointed in not hearing from you a second time before now, and as I intended to answer that expected letter, I have delayed writing for a post or two.

I hope you approve of my plan of going abroad. I never could be able to make anything of my army schemes. My father's rooted aversion would have allways prevented me from rising in that way. By falling in with his schemes, I make him easy and happy, and I have a better prospect of doing well in the world, as I will have no up-hill work, but all will go smooth. I have had a letter from my father in which he expresses much affection, and declares that he has not had so much satisfaction these four years. I wish from my heart that I may be able to make myself a Man, and to become steady and sensible in my conduct. But, alas, this miserable melancholy is allways weighing me down, and rendering me indifferent to all pursuits. For these two days past, I have been very bad (owing to thick, rainy weather) and have been viewing all things in the most dissagreeable light. I have now got relief and am pretty easy and chearfull. I sympath[ise] very heartily with your distress. It is indeed a most severe affliction. You are right in thinking that we cannot drive it away. I advise you to study it carefully. Observe its effects, and find out by what methods to render yourself tollerably easy while it lasts. What I want to do is to bring myself to that aequality of behaviour that, whether my spirits are high or low, people may see little odds upon

me. I am perswaded that when I can restrain my
flightiness and keep an even external tenour, that my
mind will attain a settled serenity. My dear friend!
do all you can to keep free of it. Mix business and
amusement, so that your mind may be allways employed and no time left for the gloomy broodings of a
distempered fancy.

My father inclines that I should pass next winter at
Utrecht and afterwards proceed to the south of Europe.
At Utrecht I am told that I shall have a most beautifull
city to live in; very genteel people to be acquainted
with; an opportunity of learning the French language,
and easy opportunity of jaunting about to the Hague,
Roterdam, and, in short, up and down all the seven
Provinces. I am also to hear the lectures on civil law,
and put myself on the plan of acquiring a habit of study
and application. Too much of that would be bad for
me. But idleness is still worse. And now, my friend,
don't you think that I am upon a better plan than
forcing myself into the Guards, in time of peace, where
I should be continaly fighting — not against the
French — but against my father's inclination? Don't
you think, too, that I am now upon a more independent
and extensive plan, and that a Man with such a mind
as I have should rather embrace soft measures? My
dear Johnston! you may figure the many spirited, gay
ideas which I entertain when I consider that I am now
a young man of fortune, just going to set out on his
travels. That time which I have often at a distance
looked forward to is arrived. My father wants to have
me go as soon as possible. So that I shall set out in a
fortnight or less.

As to my affairs, Love has payed me £10, and still owes me £30, which I believe I must allow to lie over a little. My boy's maintenance, I imagine, will come to £10 a year. I have a notion to make out three bills, each of that sum, which I will cause Love sign, payable at different future terms, and these I will indorse to you; so that you can be supplied from time to time. I am anxious to hear of Charles. Meet with Cairnie and get his accounts of him. I shall send you some journal next Tuesday. You shall hear every post from me now till I leave Britain. I ever am

Your sincere friend,
JAMES BOSWELL.

If letters went astray, as they do in the old comedies, and this one had been delivered into the hands of the Laird of Auchinleck, instead of to John Johnston of Grange, what a rumpus there would have been! From the first word to the last, this letter, despite its easy chatter, is strictly secret intelligence, by no means intended for the eye or ear of parents. "Jaunting about to the Hague and Roterdam," indeed! "Up and down all the Seven Provinces," quotha! James Boswell was being sent to Holland to read the law, and he knew it. Nothing had been said, we must believe, about those "very genteel people" he hoped to meet, and no promise had been extracted from the father by which one might be justified in asserting that it was planned that he should afterwards

"proceed" to the south of Europe. To the Laird
of Auchinleck it is all strictly practical. James is
being sent to Utrecht to acquire a professional
education; he is not being sent off on the Grand
Tour. He had wasted his time and opportunities
when he had been put to the work in Scotland,
and now some other plan must be tried. But as
for holiday junketings . . .

And now note the skill with which youth goes
at the management of parents. Nothing had come
of Boswell's proposal to get a commission in the
Guards. Part of the attractiveness of the proposal, anyhow, was that the road to a commission
led immediately to London. And then his father
had grumbled and protested from the beginning.
Dreams of martial glory must be laid aside. But
not without getting something for them. The
plan is to sell them to the father for the Grand
Tour through Europe, "proceeding" as far as
Rome, or — who knows? — Corsica. Seem to fall
in with your father's plans. The first thing to do is
to regain the parental favour. The first step toward the Grand Tour is to get a foothold on the
Continent. It is unfortunate that it must be
Utrecht, but perhaps something can be made of
Utrecht. At any rate, there will be the opportunity of learning — the French language. There are
the Seven Provinces to go jaunting about in, and,

in the distance, after a year, Italy and Rome. "I am also to hear lectures on civil law." — O Jemmy Boswell, Jemmy Boswell, O!

But before one makes off to Europe, to be gone, perhaps, three years, one settles one's private affairs; and hence this letter to the young solicitor-friend. Love has not yet paid up. Love was one of Boswell's actor-friends and former heroes, who is remembered as the man who first urged him to keep a journal. If Love should pay the thirty pounds which he still owes, the money may be applied to another object.

"My boy's maintenance, I imagine, will come to £10 a year." In the good old days of Samuel Pepys, the care of an illegitimate child "for ever" cost a man £5. Moll Flanders, it may be recalled, got rid of her child by an initial expense of £10. And now, in the year of our Lord 1763, the charge has risen to £10 annually. Or was it that Boswell, who, as we shall see later, had as much fatherly pride in his offspring as Robert Burns, had provided for his youngster some superior "accommodations"? Charles is, very probably, the name of this "boy," Cairnie, not impossibly, that of his caretaker. I cannot tell. It is now probably too late to identify them. At any rate, I have not succeeded in doing so.

"My boy's maintenance." Poor little boy!

Poor little waif flung out at random, on the great sea of life, with ten pounds a year for maintenance! What your life was, lost among the peasants of southern Scotland, who shall guess? Your lot is less distinguished than that of Wordsworth's French daughter, for no books can be written about you. But your mere existence tells us something about your father that we did not know before. His melancholy had, it is clear, a very real foundation, which has hitherto been overlooked. His pious relatives would have called it sin and the wages of sin. The young fellow, who had reached the age of twenty-two, must indeed have felt that, in enjoying the pleasures of this world, he had moved at a rather rapid pace, and that the consequences of that pace were becoming a burden. Hence the promises of reform, and the determination to become "steady and sensible" in his conduct.

And so, having settled his affairs as best might be, under circumstances not wholly satisfactory, and having brought his father to a state of mind more or less hopeful, in which he might be amenable to later proposals for James's junketing about the Seven Provinces, Germany, Switzerland, and Italy, young Boswell prepared himself to depart. A varied experience awaited him on the Continent, and an enrichment of that genius which nature had bestowed upon him. He carried his luck with him, and in the game which ensued between him and his father, — a game which was played with the Grand Tour for a stake, — fortune consistently smiled upon the son.

Jas Boswell, 1758

CHAPTER II

IN HOLLAND AND GERMANY

JAMES BOSWELL's attainments in the law have been subjected to the same slighting criticism as everything else connected with his personal life. It does not do to be too frank with regard to yourself, or you will find that the world is accepting your own estimate, or accepting it at a discount. In his Commonplace Book Boswell wrote: —

Boswell had a great aversion to the law, but forced himself to enter upon that laborious profession in compliance with the anxious desire of his father, for whom he had the greatest regard. After putting on the gown, he said with great good humour to his brother advocates, "Gentlemen, I am prest into the service here; but I have observed that a prest man, either by sea or land, after a little time does just as well as a volunteer."

Boswell never liked his profession, but he contrived (until he left Scotland) to get along in it. In youth, he never liked the reading of the law, but he contrived to do it. Indeed, we may say that he was compelled to do it. If definite proof be demanded, that proof can be supplied. Boswell's fee-book is preserved in the Advocates' Library at Edinburgh, and an examination of it will convince any one that he was a busy and successful young lawyer.

The assumption that Boswell wasted all his time in those youthful days when he was set at the reading of law is incorrect. It is caused in part by a passage in one of his very earliest letters, written, at the age of eighteen, to Temple, from Edinburgh, which for many years has circulated in the following form: —

I can assure you the study of the law here is a most laborious task. In return for yours, I shall give you an account of my studies. From nine to ten I attend the law-class; from ten to eleven study at home; and from one to two attend a college upon Roman Antiquities; the afternoon and evening I likeways spend in study.

It would seem as if a morning in which one hour was given to attending a class in law and one to studying it was no very arduous way of beginning the day. But, as a matter of fact, the first editor of the letters has carelessly dropped out a trifle of two hours. The manuscript reads: —

From 9 to 10, I attend the law class; from 10 to 11, the Astronomy; from 11 to 1, study at home; from 1 to 2, attend a college upon Roman Antiquities, etc.

Clearly, if there is any truth in this account, Boswell could not easily have failed to shuffle on some knowledge.

Dr. J. T. T. Brown, of Glasgow, who owns Boswell's annotated copy of Erskine's "Institutes," — itself an evidence of no slight industry, — has expressed himself in clear terms respecting Boswell's knowledge of the law. He is a man of profound familiarity with that unique subject, Scots law, and a Boswellian scholar of the first rank, and we can do no better than listen to his summary.

It is a mistake to suppose, as most critics do, that Boswell wholly dissipated the four years spent at Edinburgh and Glasgow Universities, and went to Utrecht ill prepared to benefit from tuition there. The opposite is true. As a student both in Edinburgh and Glasgow his name no doubt is associated with more than one wild frolic and with some self-indulgence too; but the fact that he passed his trials as a Civilian for admission to the Faculty of Advocates, a year before he left home, is enough of itself to prove the quality of his attainments. By far the greater number of aspiring advocates obtained admission by what was then called the Municipal Law examination; only a few chose the much higher pass in Civil Law. Lord Auchinleck, besides, had specially tutored his son in Roman Law and encouraged his studies in Greek so that he might when in Holland benefit by Trotz's prelections on the Theodosian Code.

There were several reasons for the choice of Utrecht as the place where Boswell should continue his legal studies. In the first place, the Dutch jurisconsults were among the most learned and influential in all Europe, so that it was a common thing for young Scottish students of the law to conclude their training in Holland. Boswell's father had himself been a student at Leyden. Moreover, Sir David Dalrymple, having been at Utrecht eighteen years before, was able to give Boswell much valuable advice respecting the work there. It was, indeed, Sir David who first suggested the university as the desirable place for the completion of Boswell's training. The young man himself would have preferred a French academy, but Sir David did not approve. Lord Auchinleck gave an easy assent to the proposals of his brother advocate, which he would almost certainly have denied to any plan originating with his son. Again, the Boswells had relatives in Holland. Boswell's great grandmother, the Countess of Kincardine, was of Dutch birth, and a member of the "noble house of Sommelsdyck." "The family," writes Boswell in the "Tour to the Hebrides," "has still great dignity and opulence, and by intermarriages is connected with many other noble families." His father gave Boswell a letter of introduction to Gronovius, a scholar with whom he had been intimate many years before, while Sir David commended him to the care of the Count of Nassau, at Utrecht, a distinguished publicist and man of letters.

We know more of Boswell's plans with respect
to Utrecht than of his attainments there. A fortnight before his departure from England, he gave
Sir David the following description of his plans : —

I am determined to study the civil law and the law of
nature and nations. I shall also have Erskine's "Institutes" with me, and by degrees acquire the Scots
law. I shall follow a plan which you once suggested to
me, of making a copy of the whole book, which will fix
my attention to the subject, and help to imprint it on
my memory. The acquiring French is a matter of
great moment, and I am determined to be very assiduous in doing so. I shall look about here for a good
French servant of undoubted character, and, at any
rate, shall have such a one at Utrecht. I shall dine at
the old "Castle of Antwerp." I am told by the same
gentleman who told me many other things, that the
new one is the best; but, as he likewise told me that
they generally spoke English, and as I have now no
great respect for his accounts, I shall be with your old
friend or his successor.

On August 5, 1763, therefore, at five o'clock in
the morning, Boswell left London *en route* for Harwich and Holland. He was accompanied by
Samuel Johnson, who was fain to show his affection for his young friend by accompanying him as
far as Harwich and the packet-boat. As readers
of the "Life of Johnson" will recall, they made a
pleasant jaunt of it, and broke the journey at Col-

chester, arriving at Harwich next day. Boswell
was a little nervous at the thought of the new life
that awaited him, and downcast at leaving the
joys of London. He tells us that he "teized" his
companion "with fanciful apprehensions of unhappiness"; and it was on this occasion that
Johnson, pointing to a moth that had burnt its
life out in a candle-flame, remarked, "That creature was its own tormentor, and I believe its name
was Boswell."

Johnson walked down to the beach with the
boy, and saw him safe on the packet-boat to Hel-
voetsluys. "As the vessel put out to sea," remarks
Boswell, "I kept my eyes upon him for a considerable time, while he remained rolling his majestic
frame in the usual manner; and at last I perceived
him walk back into the town, and he disappeared."

Upon his arrival in Utrecht, Boswell put up at
the Cour de l'Empereur; but we know nothing
more of his early days there than that he found
the town very dull, and fell into a fit of blues. But
before the year was out, social intercourse had
restored his natural gaiety. Before December
he was sufficiently intimate with his new teacher,
whom he calls "mynheer Trotz," to enlist his
assistance for Dr. Johnson in the study of the
Frisian language. Moreover, he recorded in his
Commonplace Book an anecdote narrated by

Trotz, which seems to show that the old gentleman was not without some sense of humour.

When Mr. Trotz, Professor of Civil Law at Utrecht, was at Copenhagen, he had a mind to hear the Danish pulpit oratory, and went into one of their churches. At that time the barbarous custom of making spoil of shipwrecked goods still prevailed in Denmark. The minister prayed with great fervency: "O Lord, if it please Thee to chastise the wicked for their sins, and to send forth Thy stormy winds to destroy their ships, we beg Thou mayest throw them upon our coasts rather [than] upon any other, that Thy chosen people may receive benefit therefrom, and with thankful hearts may glorify Thy holy name."

There is not sufficient evidence here to prove that our young friend had begun to Boswellise Professor Trotz — there is but a single straw to show the direction of the wind. But we know that Boswell's instincts set consistently in that quarter; and I, for one, shall not easily be convinced that this was an exception to the rule.

There were other distinguished persons with whom he established an intimacy. He was received, apparently with perfect freedom, into the family of one of the governors of the province, Baron de Zuylen, a nobleman of great wealth and distinguished lineage. Out of this association sprang one of the most amusing of the numerous love-stories which diversify the biography of Bos-

well, and which will be narrated in its proper
place. Meanwhile, it is only necessary to say here
that love was one of the means by which he contrived to get the better of that homesickness which
had afflicted him upon his arrival in Utrecht.

He also made the acquaintance, naturally, of
the Reverend William Brown, Minister of the
Scottish Church at Utrecht; but the person whose
conversation delighted him most was a young
clergyman named Charles Giffardier, with whom
he could amuse himself when in lighter mood.
This clerical gentleman was destined, many years
later, to achieve a modest reputation by his appearance in Fanny Burney's "Diary," under the
pseudonym of "Mr. Turbulent." Save for Miss
Burney's notice of him and his riotous humour,
he has no claim to remembrance. He was Queen
Charlotte's French reader when Miss Burney knew
him at court; but the glimpse we are now to have
of him shows him in close relations with the youthful Boswell nearly a quarter of a century before, at
a time when his spirits were probably no less turbulent than in middle age. He told Boswell anecdotes of French army life for him to record in his
Commonplace Book, and, in general, fascinated
him by his French assurance and gaiety. Boswell's
letter to him, which is here printed, gives us
the only reliable information which has so far

been discovered regarding Boswell's social life in Utrecht.

UTRECHT, 16 *December*, 1763.

MONSIEUR, —

By the address of this letter, you will see that I intended to write in French. By the address I mean the exordium, *Monsieur.* I did indeed fully intend to have written to you in that language, of which you know so much, and I so little. But I recollected that my French letters are as yet but mere themes, and that I should not be doing you a great kindness to give you the trouble to correct them.

Although I cannot correct the language of your letter, yet I think I may take upon me to correct the sentiment of it. Your French morality, Giffardierre, is "lighter than vanity." A generous Briton gives it to the wind, with a smile of disdain. To be serious, your amorous sentences are vivacious. But are they proper from a son of the Church? Indeed, Doctor, I am affraid not. Beleive me, Sir, such sallies are dangerous. They glance upon the mind, and dazzle the eye of discernment. Morality is permanent, altho' our sight be wavering; happy are they who can keep it constantly in view. I have experienced a good deal of variety, and I am firmly convinced that the true happiness of a MAN is propriety of conduct and the hope of divine favour. Excuse me, Giffardier, I am domineering over you, I allow. But don't you deserve it? When you left this, was you not resolved to acquire "intellectual dignity"? I desire that you may remember your resolution. You have now a fair opportunity to become a real philosopher. If you improve your solitude as you ought to do, the rest of your life may be past in chearfull tranquillity. Take this as it is meant and you will thank me.

I now find Utrecht to be the same agreable place which my freind Dalrymple found it fifteen years ago. We have brilliant assemblys twice a week and private parties allmost every evening. La Comtesse de Nassau Beverwerd has taken me under her protection. She is the finest woman upon earth. She has shown me the [grea]test civility, and has introduced me [upon] the very best footing [into the gay] world of this city. I be[gin to] make acquaintance wi[th] the people of fashion, and hope to be agreable to them. There are so many beautifull and amiable ladies in our circle that a quire of paper could not contain their praises, tho' written by a man of a much cooler fancy and a much smaller handwriting than myself.

I have stood upon my guard and have repelled dissipation. I am firm to my plan and I divide my time between study and amusement. "Happy man!" you will say. Our vacation begins this day. I shall go to the Hague next week, and expect to pass there some weeks of felicity. Do not allow yourself to weary in your present retreat. Acquire fortitude, and all will at least be supportable in this changefull world.

I am, Sir,

Your sincere well-wisher and humble servant,

JAMES BOSWELL.

Last post I had a long letter from Mr. Johnson.

There is not much here about work; but then, one does not write letters about work. To-morrow vacation begins, and our mind is filled with "gay ideas" once more; there will be "weeks of felicity." The reader will not have forgotten that, according to our hero's earliest plans, there was to be much junketing about the Seven Provinces. He had discussed his plans with Johnson, and had even gone so far as to suggest that Johnson should come over to the Low Countries in the following summer, and tour them with him. This Christmas holiday, however, shall be spent at The Hague, where, as has been said, he could claim relationship with certain aristocratic families. There was apparently no difficulty in obtaining the paternal assent to this plan, and the visit was made. He passed a fortnight in the "gay world" at The Hague, where he was graciously received by his relatives and by "many other people of distinction." Of his relatives we know nothing more; but he formed an association with a group of young Scottish advocates, among whom was William Nairne, who, a decade later, accompanied Boswell and Johnson as far as St. Andrews on the Hebridean tour. It was he whom Johnson then described as "a gentleman who could stay with us only long enough to make us know how much we lost by his leaving us." Another was Andrew Stuart, who later made a name for himself in the famous Douglas case, and fought a duel with Lord Thurlow. The three young fellows coached from The Hague to Rotterdam. Stuart seized the reins from the Dutch blockhead who held them, and showed him how a party of young Britons expected to travel. Boswell said he drove so hard that the very moles came above ground to look at him.

During this vacation he also visited Leyden, where A. Gronovius invited him to "pass a Saturday," and inspect certain notes on Greek lyric poetry. He put up at the Golden Ball, and ate his supper in the great parlour, or public room, of that inn. We get a glimpse of him from his Commonplace Book, in which he habitually refers to himself in the third person — an indication of his instinctive tendency to make drama of the simplest events of his daily life.

As he was eating a sober bit of supper, there entered three roaring West Indians, followed by a large dog. They made a deal of rude noise. The waiter thought it incumbent upon him to make an apology for their roughness. "Sir," said he, "they are very good-natured gentlemen." "Yes, yes," said Boswell, "I see they are very good-natured gentlemen, and in my opinion, sir, the dog seems to be as good-natured as any of the three."

This anecdote is certainly not worth reprinting for its wit, but it may serve as a specimen of Boswell's ability to lend to the most commonplace occurrence a vividness and actuality that were later to be reckoned among his most conspicuous endowments. In Leyden, too, he met the Honourable Charles Gordon, son of the Earl of Aberdeen, whom he invited to visit him in Utrecht. "Mr. Boswell," said Gordon, "I would willingly come and see you for a day at Utrecht, but I am afraid I should tire you." "Sir," replied Boswell, "I defy you to tire me for one day."

There is something significant in the absence from the Commonplace Book of the usual topics discussed by travellers, and the presence, instead, of such anecdotes as those just set down. Neither the canals in Holland nor the Alps in Switzerland seem to have impressed him. His indifference to architecture was complete, and the only pictures that I remember his having mentioned are the paintings found at Herculaneum, in which he felt an antiquarian rather than an artistic interest. The outward aspect of cities meant little to him. He called Berlin "a fine city," and said, at Rome, that he viewed the ancient remains with "venerable enthusiasm"; but Utrecht, Florence, Venice, Naples elicited no praise from his ordinarily enthusiastic pen. Johnson's advice may account for a measure of this indifference, for he had counselled Boswell to go where there were courts and learned men; he was "of Lord Essex's opinion, rather to go an hundred miles to speak with one wise man, than five miles to see a fair town." It was Johnson who found water "the same everywhere," and thought the Giants' Causeway "worth seeing, but not worth going to see."

Still, Boswell's indifference to scenery and to pictorial art is more than "a plume from the wing of Johnson" (as Wilkes would have called it), and these anecdotes contain the explanation. Conversation, it is to be remembered, was ever for him the purest joy in life; in travelling, it is the means of cultivating what the century loved to call "universality." The object of travel is to become a citizen of the world, rather than an *arbiter elegantiarum*. In the course of his travels, Boswell will associate with his own countrymen or not, according as he may profit by intercourse with them; for he has come abroad as a philosopher, not as a gypsy. Therefore, in learning to appreciate the civilisation of the Dutch or the Italians, he does not deem it necessary to repudiate his own country and strive to be mistaken for a native in the land where he happens to be. Buildings and canals and fortifications may be left to blear-eyed antiquarians with their tiresome pedantry. And so he recorded anecdotes and *bon mots*, not all of them clever, it is true, but, as a whole, reflecting a life crowded with human faces and memories, a life in which he had been not a mere spectator but a participant. For a biographer what training could have been better? It was to be his function to exhibit life in panoramic fulness and detail, to catch the conversation of the salon and the club, and yet to avoid the dulness of realism by plucking merely the flower of that life. These anecdotes are, as it were, his early studies, his first attempts, his sketch-book, *sein Hand zu weisen.*

Of his pride in his store of this kind he leaves us in no doubt. He tells how, years later, as he was one day writing in his "journal of conversations," General Paoli came upon him, and, noting his occupation, requested him to read something from the book. When the young man was long in selecting a specimen, Paoli taunted him: "Reason says I am a deer lost in a wood. It is difficult to find me." "I had," adds Boswell, "nothing to answer at the time, but afterwards — I forget how long — I said, 'The wood is crowded with deer. There are so many good things, one is at a loss which to choose.'" To him it was a well-spring of wisdom, free from the taint of the study; wisdom exhibiting herself as a glorified *savoir-faire* — wisdom, that is, in its actual application to life by men of the keenest minds. Conversation, he asserted, which could be remembered and recorded, was like the rich freight which one brings home from a journey that has been profitable as well as pleasant.

The Christmas vacation was followed by another term, and that, in due course, by the summer holidays; and it was clear to Boswell that it was time for him to be gone from among the Dutch. The time had come to "proceed" to the glorious south. But how was it to be managed?

At this moment luck favoured him once more. Late in June there returned from Scotland to the Continent a man the romance of whose early years had been equalled by the exalted station which he had attained in his age. This was George Keith, the Earl Marischal of Scotland, the intimate friend of Voltaire and Rousseau, the favourite and trusted adviser of Frederick the Great. In youth he had twice been out campaigning for the Stuarts, and had found it well, after the failure of the campaign of 1719, to live abroad. He came under the protection of the King of Prussia, whose personal ambassador he was at the courts of France and of Spain. Upon his communication of valuable political intelligence to William Pitt, he was pardoned by George II, as that monarch was nearing the end of his life. The Earl returned to Scotland for a time. He was now nearly seventy years old, and had probably made up his mind to end his days in his native land. During this residence he met Lord Auchinleck, with whom he became inti-

mate. He had served, in youth, under the Earl of
Mar, a relative of Mrs. Boswell. But his peaceful
retirement was interrupted in the spring of 1764,
when he was urgently invited by his Prussian master to return to Potsdam. This he agreed to do.

Now, just at this time Lord Auchinleck was in
doubt — as usual — regarding the best course to
pursue with his son James. The boy was eager to
travel and see life. Beyond a doubt, the matter
was laid before the Earl Marischal, and a decision
reached that young Boswell was to visit the German courts, and to travel in the company of the
Earl as far as Berlin. To Lord Auchinleck it
must have seemed a safe and happy solution of
a pressing problem.

Lord Keith left England on the seventh of June,
and was in company with a young Turkish lady,
Emetulla by name, who appears in Boswell's notes
as "Mademoiselle Ameté, the Turk." She was the
Earl's adopted daughter, a lady whom his brother,
General Keith, is said to have rescued at the siege
of Oczakow.

At some spot or other, then, in the Low Countries or in Western Germany, Boswell joined the
Earl and his fair charge, and a remarkable trio
they must have been: the venerable diplomat,
who was received with all possible attention where-
ever the party stopped; the silent Turkish lady,

and the eager young traveller, who was at last on
the wing. That Boswell undertook to collect
materials for an intimate sketch of the Earl
Marischal is certain. He promised Rousseau that,
on his return from Corsica, he would show him a
"portrait," that is, a character-sketch, with anecdotes and reminiscences of the Earl Marischal,
who was now old and likely soon to pass away.
One anecdote recorded in the Commonplace Book
takes us far back, to the days of the Old Pretender
and the uprising of 1715, when Lord Keith was an
officer of cavalry.

In the year 1715, Lord Marischal observed a Highlander crying, and looking at the poor fellow, he observed he had no shoes. He sent one to him, who
spoke Erse, and bid him not to be cast down, for he
should have shoes. "Sir," said the Highlander, "I
want no shoes; I am crying to see a Macdonald retire
from his enemy."

As for the Earl, he was amazed at his new friend,
who confided to him the most remarkable notions.
Some months later he wrote to Rousseau, "Boswell
is a very fine fellow, but full of hypochondriac and
visionary ideas. He has often seen spirits. I do
hope that he will not fall into the hands of people
who will turn his head completely."
The little party reached Berlin on July 7, and

two days later Boswell wrote to Mademoiselle de
Zuylen in Utrecht:—

I have had a most agreeable journey. My Lord
Marischal was most entertaining company, and the
Turkish lady talked extremely well when indolence
did not keep her in silence. We were very happy at
Brunswic. I have been only two days at Berlin. But
I see that much happiness awaits me in this beautifull
capital. The German formality and state pleases me
much, for I am the true old Scots Baron.

In this short quotation there is much that is worthy
of notice. The young Turkish lady, for example,
seems to be inadequately described. She had no
conversation. How, therefore, was a Boswell to
record her adequately? She had, apparently, an
Oriental indolence, but not the vivacity of Mademoiselle de Zuylen, to whom he was writing.

It would be interesting to know if Boswell saw,
or tried to see, King Frederick. German princes
he certainly did meet and converse with, as he was
careful later to narrate. But he was soon to weary
of German etiquette. As the young friend of the
Earl Marischal, all doors were open to him, and he
saw what there was to see. He went to Charlot-
tenberg on the occasion of the betrothal of the
Princess of Brunswick to the Prince of Prussia,
but found nothing worthy of record except a *mot*
of his own. He was presented to the British

envoy, Andrew Mitchell, in whose conversation,
he avers, he found "uncommon pleasure." The
envoy had, apparently, listened with patience to
the young fellow, and then given him some good
advice.

To Mitchell Boswell wrote a couple of letters
which have been reprinted as often as any that he
ever wrote. They have been laid under contribu-
tion by those who enjoy scolding at Boswell, for
they are, indeed, very impudent letters. It had
occurred to Boswell that he might "use" the
British envoy. Might it not be possible to prevail
on him to write to Lord Auchinleck and recommend that James be permitted to make the Italian
tour? It was a peculiarly Boswellian scheme, of
the sort which he had before this carried success-
fully into execution. Had not Sir David Dalrymple interceded with his father on the boy's
behalf? And so he confided to Mitchell that the
"words of the Apostle Paul, 'I must see Rome,'
had been strongly *borne in*" upon his mind! He
explained that he had passed a year in Utrecht,
where he had recovered his "inclination for study
and rational thinking." Now he is ready for his
travels; but his father's views are unfortunately
"entirely different": he thinks that James had
better go back to Utrecht for another winter.
Clearly it is not that the father merely objects to

the boy's absence from Scotland another year.
Cannot Lord Auchinleck be made to realise that
his son intends to travel through Italy, not as a
"Mi Lord Anglois," but as a scholar and a "man
of elegant curiosity"? Surely, if Mr. Mitchell
would be so kind as to explain to Lord Auchinleck,
all would be well. "I would beg, Sir," he says,
"that you may write to my father your opinion as
to this matter, and put it in the light which you
may think it deserves." The father had gone so
far as to consent to a visit to Paris; surely, surely
it is not beyond hope that he will consent to Italy
also.

Can the reader believe that Mr. Mitchell was so
hard-hearted as to decline this ingenuous request?
It is the business of envoys to give cautious advice,
and to avoid becoming a catspaw. Mitchell acted
like a true envoy, and wrote to Boswell that he
would do well to obey his father. Obviously.
But the advice came too late. Lord Auchinleck
had already yielded, and Boswell could not resist
the temptation to triumph over the envoy : —

You tell me gravely to follow the plan which my
father prescribes, whatever it may be, as in doing so,
I shall certainly act most wisely. I forgive you this;
for I say just the same to young people whom I advise.
. . . I have, however, the happiness to inform you that
my father has consented that I shall go to Italy.

He wrote this letter after he had left Germany. Five months had passed, and it was again the Christmas season. Our young traveller had "proceeded" as far as Geneva, and had, indeed, already met Rousseau. Life was opening up to him. Life is what you choose to make it. The world is one's oyster. As for the game which he had been playing with his father, it was now over, and youth had won. Those who have not forgotten their own youth may be able to pardon the boy for obviously, and a little impudently, relishing his triumph.

CHAPTER III

WITH THE FRENCH PHILOSOPHERS

THE winter of 1764 and 1765 has hitherto been almost a blank page in the biography of Boswell; but with the aid of his letters to Rousseau, which have never been published or even read over by scholars, but copies of which have, by great good fortune, come into my hands, we are enabled to tell in outline the story of his life during this period, and to see the influence of events in fixing the literary ambitions of him who was to be the Prince of Biographers.

Boswell departed from Germany, then, disgusted with courts, and repining at the dearth of great men in that country, went to Switzerland. He went first to the Val de Travers, where he proposed to meet Rousseau. He had decided to approach him with no other recommendation than his own social genius. Now, inasmuch as this was not, in general, Boswell's method of approach to a great man, we are justified, I think, in assuming that he had failed to find anyone who would give him the necessary letter of introduction. Lord Keith might have done it, but he knew Rousseau all too well to care to do it. It is clear that he explained to Boswell that Rousseau was living in retreat from the world and denying himself to all visitors. Boswell had better give up the attempt to meet him. But the young Scot was not easily discouraged. He had never yet failed to meet anyone whom he had made up his mind to meet. There must be ways of prevailing even upon a Rousseau. There are a thousand kinds of appeal that may be made to a philosopher: one might, for example, rest one's case on one's dire need of spiritual counsel. It is only necessary to show a philosopher that one is a worthy disciple, that one has lived a life not unlike that of the master. And so the artful creature composed the following letter, which I render into English, since it is somewhat difficult to see the implications of Boswell's tortured French phrases.

VAL DE TRAVER, 3 *December* 1764.

MONSIEUR, —

I am a gentleman of an old Scotch family [*un ancien gentilhomme écossois*]. You know my rank. I am twenty-four years old. You know my age. It is sixteen months since I left Great Britain, completely insular, knowing hardly a word of French. I have been in Holland and in Germany, but not yet in France. You will therefore excuse my language. I am on my travels, and have a genuine desire to perfect myself. I have come here in the hope of seeing you.

I have heard, Sir, that it is difficult to meet you [*que vous êtes fort difficile*] and that you have refused the visits of several persons of the highest distinction. For that, Sir, I respect you all the more. If you were to receive everyone who came to you just to be able to say boastingly, "I have seen him," your house would no longer be the retreat of exquisite Genius nor of elevated Piety; and I should not be enthusiastically eager to be received there.

I present myself, Sir, as a man of unique merit, as a man with a sensitive heart, a spirit lively yet melancholy. Ah! if all I have suffered gives me no special merit in the eyes of M. Rousseau, why was I ever so created, and why did he ever write as he has done [*a-t-il tellement écrit*]?

Do you ask me for letters of recommendation? Is there need of any with a man like you? An introduction is necessary in the world of affairs, in order to protect those who have no insight for impostors. But, Sir, can you, who have studied human nature, be deceived in a man's character? My idea of you is this: aside from the unknowable essence of the human soul, you have a perfect knowledge of all the principles of body and mind; their actions, their sentiments, in short, of whatever they can accomplish or acquire in the way of influence over man. In spite of all this, Sir, I dare to present myself before you. I dare to submit myself to the proof. In cities and in courts where there is a numerous society, it is possible to disguise one's self; it is possible even to dazzle the eyes of the greatest philosophers. But I put myself to the severest proof. It is in the silence and the solitude of your hallowed retreat that you shall judge of me; think you that in such circumstances I should be capable of dissimulation?

Your writings, Sir, have softened my heart, raised my spirits, and kindled my imagination. Believe me, you will be glad to see me. You know Scotch pride. Sir, I come to you to make myself worthy to belong to a nation that has produced a Fletcher of Saltoun, and an Earl Marischal. Pardon me, Sir, but I am moved! I can no longer refrain myself. O beloved St. Preux! Inspired Mentor! Eloquent and amiable Rousseau! I have a presentiment that a noble friendship is to be born this day.

I learn with great regret, Sir, that you are frequently indisposed. You may be so at present; but I implore you not to let that prevent your receiving me. You will find in me a simplicity which will in no wise disturb you and a cordiality which may assist you in forgetting your pains.

I have much to say to you. Although but a young man, I have had a variety of experiences, with which you will be impressed. I am in serious and delicate circumstances, and am most ardently desirous of having the counsels of the author of "La Nouvelle Héloïse." If you are the benevolent man that I think you, you will not hesitate to bestow them upon me. Open your door, then, Sir, to a man who dares to say that he deserves to enter there. Trust a unique foreigner. You will never repent it. But, I beg of you, be alone. In spite of my enthusiasm, after having written you in this manner, I am not sure that I would not rather forego seeing you than meet you for the first time in company. I await your reply with impatience.

BOSWELL.

Who could refuse such a request? Certainly not
Jean Jacques Rousseau. Apparently the interview
came off exactly as Boswell desired it. From
remarks in later letters and hints dropped here
and there, it is possible to reconstruct the general
scheme of their association. Since romantic melancholy had become, thanks to Rousseau, the
fashionable pose, Boswell told of the tempera-
mental gloom that frequently descended upon him;
of the hypochondria that had afflicted him in
Utrecht. (It is noteworthy that with Boswell, as
with ourselves, the sharpest fits of melancholia
were coincident with confinement in harness.) He
told him all this, and elicited from Rousseau the
compliment which he never tired of quoting: "Il y
a des points où nos âmes sont liés."

He told him, moreover, of his affairs of the heart,
and explained that he was in doubt with regard to
his latest flame, Mlle. Isabella de Zuylen (whom he
called "Zélide"), as being the final choice of his
heart. He sent him a sketch of his own life, —
which would be worth its weight in gold to-day if
it could be turned up, — in order that the great
man might be thoroughly acquainted with his new
friend. They conversed about the Earl Marischal,
and Boswell proposed to write a "Portrait" (as it
was called in the salons) or character-sketch of him.
(It would appear that Rousseau's genius recog-

nized the youngster's fitness for this kind of composition.) He got a promise from him of a letter to his philosophic friend, De Leyre, the librarian of the Duke of Parma, destined to achieve a certain prominence in the French Revolution — a man whose acquaintance Boswell promptly cultivated in Italy.

He begged Rousseau to correspond with him. He demanded his advice with regard to the employment of his time in Italy. Inasmuch as Rousseau was a musician, Boswell, in the third of his letters, discovered in himself a penchant for that art. He tells Rousseau that he likes to sing, confesses that he plays a bit on the flute, but that he despises it. Here was a sorry blunder: he did not know that Rousseau himself was addicted to playing the flute. It is our loss that he did not know it, for he would never have failed to expatiate on so important a bond between them. Some two years before, he had tried the violin, but found it a difficult instrument and gave it up. "Tell me, would it not be well for me to apply myself seriously to music — up to a certain point? Tell me which instrument I should take up. It is late, I admit; but should I not have the pleasure of making continous progress, and — " But it is no longer fair to conceal from the reader the *ipsissima verba* of the French original: "Ne serais-je pas capable d'adoucir ma vieillesse par les sons de ma lyre?" The vision of James Boswell in the rôle of Ossian, with white beard streaming to the winds, amid the romantic glades of Auchinleck, soothing his stricken age with a lyre, is one that no kindly imagination will reject.

But Rousseau was more than a musician, more than a philosopher retired from the world. He was a teacher of conduct, and his influence had long since been felt as a force in the daily lives of men. Therefore Boswell submits to him a practical question of morals. He cites, with a vividness of narrative that was later to become the most distinguished of his literary qualities, an *affaire d'honneur* in which he had become involved the summer before, and from which he had escaped with more skill than glory. I give it without abbreviation.

Last summer in Germany I found myself in the midst of a large company, a company very disagreeable to me and in which I was sorry to be losing my time. The talk was all in praise of the French. Thereupon I declaimed against that nation in the rudest terms. An officer rose, came to my side and said, "Monsieur, I am a Frenchman, and none but a scoundrel would speak as you have done of that nation." We were still at dinner. I made him a bow. I had half an hour for reflection. After dinner I led the captain out into the garden. I said to him, "Sir, I am greatly embarrassed. I have

been very impolite. I am sincerely sorry. But you
have made use of a word which a man of honour cannot
endure, and I must have satisfaction. If it be possible
to avoid a quarrel, I should be delighted, for I was in the
wrong. Will you be so good as to beg my pardon before
the company? I will first beg yours. If you cannot
agree to my proposal, we must fight, although I admit
to you that I shall do so with repugnance." I addressed
him with the *sang-froid* of a philosopher determined to
do his duty. The officer was a fine fellow. He said to
me, "Sir, I will do as you wish." We returned to the
company, and made our apologies, one to the other.
We embraced. The affair was ended. I could not,
however, rest content without consulting two or three
Scotsmen. I said to them, "Gentlemen, I am a simple
man. I am not in touch with your social rules, but I
believe that I have acted like a man. You are my com-
patriots. I ask your advice." They assured me that
the affair had been honourably adjusted between us.
They advised me to take this experience as a lesson for
the future.

But still the young man's mind is not at rest.
He charges himself at times with cowardice —
"Je suis d'un tempérament craintif." The philosopher's opinion is sought. "What do you seriously think of duels?" There is the peculiarly
Boswellian touch, the conscious art of the interviewer disguising itself under the mask of *naïveté*.
In dealing with Boswell, nothing is easier than to
let our attention dwell on his apparent simplicity,

or vanity, or even folly, to the point of entirely
missing the thing that he would be at. What
Rousseau happens to think about Boswell's valor
in this particular incident is, of course, of strictly
secondary importance compared with the primary
intention of getting the great man to express himself. One may sacrifice a great deal of personal
esteem if one can draw forth from Rousseau a dis-
sertation on duelling. And so Boswell adds to the
question I have quoted this skillful observation:
"You have not said enough of the matter in your
'Héloïse.' There are people who think that the
Gospel teaches us to be too supine in this regard."
Clearly the young man has prepared the ground.
If Rousseau replies at all, he can hardly avoid the
expression of his views on duelling, and the pages
of Boswell's note-book (and of his future "Reminiscences of Rousseau") will be enriched with a
unique morsel.

But the ending of this third letter from which I
have been quoting is, in truth, one of the most
delightful and characteristic bits that our biographical adventurer ever penned. His busy mind
had discovered yet another avenue of approach to
the retired sage, which would lead (could one but
get started upon it) straight into the domestic
privacies of life which Boswell so dearly prized.
Obviously one means of approach to a man is

through his mistress.   Therefore Boswell ends his
letter thus: "You will not take offense if I write
occasionally to Mlle. Vasseur.   I swear that I have
no intention of carrying off your duenna [*d'enlever
votre gouvernante*].   I sometimes form romantic
plans; never impossible plans."

What reply — if any — Jean Jacques made to
this attractive proposal, I cannot tell.   Nor, alas,
have any letters from Boswell to Thérèse Le Vasseur as yet rewarded my search.   But certain it
is that the proposal gave no offence.   For when,
some thirteen months later, Rousseau crossed the
Channel to England, he went in company with his
philosophic friend, David Hume, and entrusted
Thérèse to the care of Boswell, who crossed some
weeks later.

But there was another philosophic retreat for our
young enthusiast to penetrate — Ferney.   There
dwelt a man who interested him no less than Rousseau — Voltaire, now in his seventy-first year, but
brilliant still, brilliant as a meteor which, with
fear of change, perplexes monarchs.   Just how the
genial young tuft-hunter got into the presence, we
cannot tell; but it is probable that he brought a
letter of introduction from the Earl Marischal,
who must have had less scruple about exposing
Voltaire to the Boswellian bacillus than the hypochondriac Rousseau.   Be this as it may, Boswell

was received, and by his own statement — and he was not given to inaccuracy — spent an hour with the aged philosopher, in conversation *tête-à-tête*.

Can you imagine the scene — the withered but still sinister Son of the Morning, with his satirical smile and his benevolent eye, confronting the busy, inquisitive, entertaining young Scot? "It was," says Boswell in describing the interview to Rousseau, "a most serious conversation. He talked of his natural religion in a striking manner." James, you see, had introduced the subject of religion — doubtless by means of citing his own infidelities. Already he has in mind an account of his discussion with Voltaire which shall correct the popular impression of him as devoid of the religious instinct.

After Voltaire had talked for a time, the young man said to himself, — and on the principle that James Boswell uttered whatever came into his head, I do not scruple to assert that he cried aloud, — "Aut Erasmus, aut diabolus!" In discussing his favourite theme of the nature of the soul, Boswell asked Voltaire a question which well indicates the skill with which he ensnared his destined prey, and which, indeed, has a very modern ring to it. "I asked him if he could give me any notion of the situation of our ideas which we have totally forgotten at the time, yet shall afterwards recollect. He paused, meditated a little, and acknowledged his ignorance in the spirit of a philosophical poet, by repeating, as a very happy allusion, a passage in Thomson's 'Seasons': 'Aye,' said he, '"Where sleep the winds when it is calm?"'"

Of course he got Voltaire to express an opinion of Rousseau; and tells us, in his "Tour to Corsica," that the older philosopher consistently spoke of the younger with a "satirical smile." Yet Boswell let his romantic imagination (as he would have called it) play with the notion of bringing the two men together, and even had the temerity to say to Rousseau, "In spite of all that has happened, you would have loved him that evening." An astute remark, which may lead to much. For, if Rousseau replies to the letter, he may assent to this pious opinion or he may reject it, but in either case there begins new matter for a biographer. As we know, neither James Boswell nor anybody else reconciled the two philosophers; but James, I regret to say, did something to increase the asperity between them. In the spring of 1776, after Rousseau had quarrelled with his English friends, Boswell designed and published a "ludicrous print," into which he introduced his three philosophical friends, Rousseau, Hume, and Voltaire. Rousseau in the shaggy attire of a "wild man" (as conceived in the reign of George III) occupies the

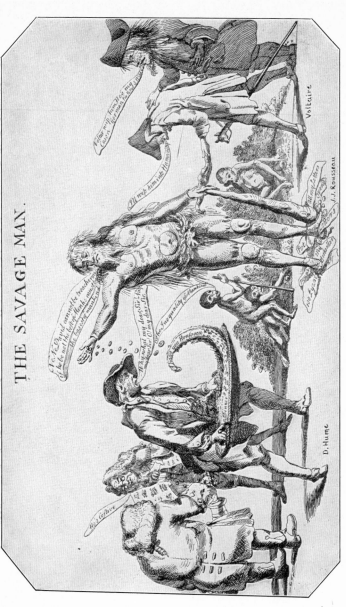

The Savage Man

Caricature of Rousseau, the Apostle of Nature, with Hume and Voltaire

A contemporary engraving, based on an original sketch by James Boswell

centre of the picture, while Voltaire smiles cynically
in the background, as one of the bystanders cries
out, "Wip 'im, Voltaire!"

On New Year's Day, 1765, James Boswell departed from Geneva, in search of new worlds to
conquer and other great men to record. He had
come into conjunction with two of the major
planets of the literary heavens. He had filled
note-books with his accounts of their conversation
—notebooks whose loss the world will long deplore.
He passed from Geneva to Turin with his social
and anecdotical soul aflame, rapt away, one fancies,
in a vision of all the glory that might be his.

On the tenth of January, he learned that John
Wilkes, in political exile from his native land, was,
for the moment, in Turin. At once he prepared
himself for the attack. O reader, do you perchance know the ballet of "Tamar"? If you do,
you will recall the close of that vivid drama.
Tamar, having finished off one victim, beholds
from her window, as she sinks back into momentary
ease, the approach of another wayfarer. She lifts
herself from cushioned luxury, and beckons to him
afar. And so the piece ends as it had begun. Or
are you, perchance, a reader of M. Benoît's sultry
romance, "L'Atlantide"? If so, you will recall
the cruel loveliness of the princess, whose malign
ambition is to surround herself with the glistening

images of her lovers, preserved for ever, actual yet golden.   Now such a passion as that of Tamar or the Atlantide possessed the innocent soul of James Boswell, biographer.   It is a paltry business to think of him as a parasite who attacked but a single victim.   Nay, rather, his was the golden hand of the realist who preserves human life in its actuality, yet ever at its best and fullest.   And if it be that there mingled with his vision of an Atlantidean circle of the golden great a baser ambition to shine in the reflected light of his splendid victims, who shall begrudge it him?   Is not the artist worthy of his fame?

And so John Wilkes, demagogue, "Apostle of Liberty," esteemed the wittiest and the most dangerous man of his day, comes within James Boswell's ken.   He is not to be won as were the philosophers.   Our artist, however, knows many wiles, and the approach which he will make in this case will be of a quite different kind.   But that, to make use of a time-honored phrase, *is another story*.

[NOTE. In a letter from Horace Walpole to Thomas Gray, written not long after Boswell's encounters with the French philosophers, a pertinent reference to the interviewer's methods, and their effect upon at least one of the interviewed, may be found.

"Pray read the new account of Corsica; what relates to Paoli will amuse you much. The author, Boswell, is a strange being, and, like Cambridge, has a rage for knowing anybody that was ever talked of. He forced himself upon me in spite of my teeth and my doors, and I see he has given a foolish account of all he could pick up from me. . . . He then took an antipathy to me on Rousseau's account, abused me in the newspapers, and expected Rousseau to do so too; but as he came to see me no more, I forgave him the rest. I see he is now a little sick of Rousseau himself, but I hope it will not cure him of his anger to me; however, his book will amuse you."]

CHAPTER IV

BOSWELL AND WILKES

THE name of John Wilkes has come down to posterity vague, to be sure, but with a definite connotation of evil. There is about it, as there is about that of Paine, a suspicion of brimstone and demagogy. It is derived, perhaps, from that cruel sketch by Hogarth, in which Wilkes is depicted as his enemies saw him, hideously cross-eyed and with his heavy sensual mouth twisted into an evil sneer. The artist has contrived to do more than set down in his hard outlines the impression of Wilkes's physical deformity: he has interpreted it as the outward mark of an obliquity of character.

The evil that Wilkes did has lived after him. And yet, if any man of the century had a right to hope that he would survive his contemporary reputation, and be thought of as playing no mean part in the development of British freedom, that man was John Wilkes. With the attempt on the part of George III to drive him out of Parliament we may, in truth, read the story of the last open attempt to exalt the prerogative of the crown over the right of the people to choose their own representatives in the House of Commons. It would seem as if

John Wilkes

Hogarth's engraving, from a portrait of his own, showing the issues of the
North Briton, of which Number 17 contained Wilkes's attack upon the painter
and Number 45 led to Wilkes's imprisonment in the Tower

Wilkes might have been remembered as one who, in winning the devotion of the common people and the personal enmity of his King, had vindicated a great principle of English liberty; but his reputation was against him. He was a gay profligate. He contrived, in the course of a long career, to outrage every tradition of British respectability. He was a free-thinker, a disloyal husband, and a wit. He delighted in wine and in revelry, and purveyed foul literature among his friends. He was suspected, not without some justice, of using his appeal for British liberty to advance his personal interests. He had an obvious delight in the mischief which he caused, and employed his political sagacity to show his friends how close he could sail to the wind. It was impossible, however, to belittle his general attractiveness, for he had demonstrated his physical courage upon the field of honour, and retained his good spirits and his wit while shut up in prison. He was a man of education, genuinely interested in the classics, and ambitious of becoming an historian. He was a loving father and a devoted friend. He could win over an enemy by his courtesy and his wit. In short, he was a man of whom respectable British folk could make nothing at all.

It was in the spring of 1763 that Wilkes faced the first great crisis of his political life. He was at the time one of the Whig leaders of the opposition, against the young King and his Prime Minister, Lord Bute. Bute, who was thought to be the tool of the King's mother, had the additional misfortune of being a Scot. The people of England had not yet forgotten the days of '45 and the Scottish devotion to the Young Pretender, and Bute had proved himself unable to dispel the national prejudice. He had, it is true, sought to establish the popularity of his government by means of the journalist and the pamphleteer. One of these, Smollett, had established a paper entitled "The Briton," which existed to spread Bute's policy of royal aggrandisement. Wilkes saw an opportunity to establish a rival journal, which should play upon the national dislike of the Scots, and rouse the people against the influences to which the King had committed himself and the Tory party. He challenged Smollett and the supporters of "The Briton" by naming his own journal, with characteristic impudence, "The North-Briton." It became notorious for its free speech and its personal invective; but results proved the efficacy of the weapons which he had chosen. In April Bute resigned. Wilkes at once brought "The North-Briton" to an end.

The succeeding Prime Minister was George Grenville, a man of feeble powers and stubborn

character, whose policies, as soon as they were announced, proved to be as offensive to Wilkes and
his party as those of his predecessor had been.
Grenville's policies, which disgusted Wilkes as
much as Bute's had done, were set before Parliament by King George in the initial "speech from
the throne." Wilkes put forth a new issue of "The
North-Briton," numbering it, consecutively with
the preceding issues, 45. In this paper, though
Wilkes was as violent as ever in the language which
he employed, he was careful to guard himself by
the assertion that the royal address was always to
be looked upon as the speech of the ministry. The
King, he remarked, was "responsible to his people
for the due exercise of the royal functions, in the
choice of his minister, &c., equal with the meanest
of subjects in his particular duty." Such language
did not please the young King and his new minister, and they proceeded at once to move against
Wilkes. A "general warrant," that is, a warrant
for the arrest and imprisonment of anyone who has
fallen under the suspicion of the bearer, was rashly
issued by Lord Halifax. It was the intention to
shut Wilkes up in the Tower and to bring him to
trial for sedition. Wilkes, who seems at no time to
have lost sight of the amusing aspect of what was
going on, eluded his captors for a time, did what he
could to destroy or spoil the evidence against him,

and then permitted himself to be taken. He was
at once committed to the Tower.

There ensued a period of the utmost excitement.
Here was a flagrant abuse of the principle of the
liberty of the subject. Were the free-born to be
hurled into prison at the whim of the House of
Hanover? And yet were all these solemn principles of English freedom to be invoked on behalf
of a libertine who had spoken lightly of sacred
majesty? What was to become of British decorum
and the ceremonial which Englishmen are scrupulous in paying to their elected monarch? Yet
Wilkes had been clapped into prison by a display
of power as tyrannical as that of a Persian despot.
No prisoner of the Bastille was more unjustly in-
carcerated. What was to be done? As usual,
matters were patched up — for the moment. On
May 6, Wilkes was brought before the Court of
Common Pleas, and, after a hearing, discharged,
on the ground that the privilege of Parliament
extended to his case, and that he ought never to
have been arrested. But it was clear to all the
world that the prisoner had been released as a
privileged person, and that his vindication was by
no means complete. Wilkes emerged with a tre-
mendously increased reputation — a problem to
his party, a thorn in the side of the King, and the
idol of the crowd. It was at this moment, when

Wilkes's name was on every lip, when his every word and every act were watched with the most anxious care by all who had the good of the nation at heart, that young James Boswell, just out of leading-strings, determined to make his acquaintance.

The two had little enough in common. Wilkes was a Whig; Boswell was a Tory, and a Tory who had an instinctive sympathy with the most extravagant claims of royalty. Wilkes, though a nominal adherent of the English Church, was a free-thinker. Boswell was a Christian and longed to be a Catholic. Wilkes, unlike Boswell, was no respecter of persons. Moreover, he affected, in particular, a contempt of Scots. But all this was no let to Boswell. He declined to take seriously the older man's dislike of his race; at worst, it but emphasised the necessity of showing him how metropolitan a Scotsman might be. In all his later relations with Wilkes, Boswell kept his nationality to the fore, so that in time Wilkes came to call him "my old Lord of Scotland," and said he looked as if he had a thousand men at his back.

But it was the gaiety of Wilkes that appealed especially to Boswell. It was clear to him that Wilkes, with all his eminence, never forgot to "shine," never forgot that social intercourse with the world of wit was the goal of human endeavour.

Here was the link between them. Here was the
method of approach. "I glory in being an enthusiast for my king and for my religion, and I
scorn the least appearance of dissimulation," he
wrote to him after the establishment of their intimacy. "As the gay John Wilkes, you are most
pleasing to me. . . . Let serious matters be out
of the question, and you and I can perfectly har-
monise." In one respect Boswell knew that he
was the equal of Wilkes — in impudence. He
would show that he knew as well as another how
to deal with a gay dog. An attitude of trembling
reverence is not the way to win a boon companion,
and therefore of this rôle in his repertory Boswell
made no use in his relations with Wilkes. He
showed him from the beginning that he was not
dazzled; and the great man, like many another,
responded instinctively to the genial youth who
dared to show that he was not afraid of him.

The immediate occasion of Boswell's first meeting with Wilkes is, unhappily, unknown. It must
have occurred about the time of the first meeting
with Johnson. At any rate, by July, 1763, their
association was well under way, and Boswell had
begun to collect anecdotes about Wilkes. "I must
tell you a joke on Wilkes," he writes to Sir David
Dalrymple. "He was coming out of Ranelagh
some nights ago, and the footmen were bawling

out, 'Mr. Wilkes's coach! Mr. Wilkes's coach!'
Lord Kelly run to the door, and cried, 'Mr. Wilkes's
coach, No. 45!' — a number which had long since
become infamous from its association with Wilkes
and the 'North-Briton.'"

But it was unfortunately necessary to interrupt
the collection of anecdotes, and obey the paternal
commands to go abroad and study the law.   Moreover, Wilkes was himself on the point of leaving
England. "I told him," writes Boswell to Sir
David Dalrymple, "I was to be in Utrecht next
winter. He said, 'If you will write to me in
George Street, I will send you the detail of this
country.' This was very obliging. It would be a
vast treasure." At this point Boswell remembers
that he is writing to an older man whose political
opinions were far from radical, and adds dutifully,
"But I don't know if it would be proper to keep
a correspondence with a gentleman in his present
capacity. It was a great honour to me his offering
it. I must be proud. Advise me fully about it."

And so the separation between the two took
place; but there was no opportunity for Boswell to
acquire the vast treasure of a weekly detail of the
news of Great Britain. As soon as the House of
Commons convened in the following November,
the attack upon Wilkes was renewed, and he had
no rest until the end of the year, when he once more

left England for France.   In January he was ex-
pelled from the House, and a month later was
found guilty in the courts of having printed No.
45 of "The North-Briton."   As he did not return
to England to receive his sentence, he was declared
an outlaw.

Such was, roughly, the posture of events in 1764,
while Boswell was studying in Utrecht and, later,
travelling in Germany.   But there are two events
in the personal life of Wilkes which it is necessary
to mention, if we are to understand the relations
between the two men when they were reëstablished
at the beginning of the following year.   Wilkes had
fallen in love with an Italian courtesan, named
Gertrude Corradini, and had lived with her for a
long time in Paris.   At the end of the year 1764
they separated, Corradini travelling in state (at
Wilkes's expense) to her home in Italy, where he
was planning to join her in January.   The journey
of the pair of them across France and Italy savours
a little of flight and pursuit — a relation between
them   which   presently   became   obvious.   But,
though Wilkes had given himself over to pleasure,
he was far from happy.   He had expected to have
the companionship, during the winter, of his devoted friend, the poet Churchill; and, indeed,
Churchill had actually joined him at Boulogne in
the previous October.   But he had been almost

immediately attacked by a fever, and had lived but a few days. Perhaps no event in the life of Wilkes touched him more deeply than this. In so far as his nature was capable of love, he had loved Churchill, and the loss of him he never ceased to lament.

When, therefore, Wilkes arrived in Turin, early in the month of January, he was still cast down by his recent bereavement; he was, furthermore, in a state of intense annoyance at his mistress. The agreement between them had been to meet at Turin; but Corradini, on arrival, had complained of rheumatism, and made off, leaving word for Wilkes that she had gone on to Bologna. At this moment, luck brought James Boswell also to Turin. He at once made overtures to Wilkes by dispatching a letter to him in which he proposed that they should dine together. This is the first of the letters of Boswell addressed to Wilkes that has come down to us, and it is, for several reasons, a curious document. Its tone of mingled good fellowship and impudence is a plain revelation of Boswell's manner when with Wilkes, and is in the most surprising and significant contrast to the attitude of cringing servility which he is commonly supposed to have adopted. But the letter piques our interest for a totally different reason. The writing on one half of the page has, unfortunately,

been obliterated. The letter, which is in the
British Museum, is one of a group deposited there
with other important papers of John Wilkes. The
packet of Boswell's letters has at some time or
other been wetted, and the top sheets seriously injured. All that can be read of the first page is
this : —

> Sir,
>   I am to
> is now in Turin.
> my monarchical
> As a Scotsman
> As a Freind I
> a companion I lo
> it is not decent fo
> him : yet I wish
> I shall be alone,
> dinner upon my ta
> If Mr. Wilkes chus
> Guest, I shall by
> it.   I may venture
> be very wellcome,
> him a feast of mo
> and choice Conversa
>   Bos
> Turin, 10 January 1765.

When I first came across this letter, I was reminded of the fragmentary document in "Monte
Cristo" that assisted Edmond Dantès in his escape

from the Château d'If. By dint of measuring
lines, and holding the sheet up to the light to study
the position of vague upward strokes of otherwise
obliterated words, it is possible to guess at the half-
lines that the water has washed away, and to reconstruct a letter which, if not a reliable repro-
duction of the original, at least makes clear sense.
I think we may take it as a fairly close approxima-
tion to the general drift of the original.

> SIR,
>   I am told that Mr. Wilkes
> is now in Turin.   I assure you that
> my monarchical soul is roused.
> As a Scotsman, I abhor him.
> As a Freind, I value him.   As
> a companion I love him, and altho
> it is not decent for me to ask him,
> yet I wish much to see him.
> I shall be alone this evening, with
> dinner upon my table for two.
> If Mr. Wilkes chuses to be my
> Guest, I shall by no means resent
> it.   I may venture to add that he will
> be very wellcome, and to promise
> him a feast of most excellent wine
> and choice Conversation.
>   BOSWELL.
> TURIN, 10 *January*, 1765.

Wilkes, it would appear, declined this invitation.
The letter which follows this one is also frag-

mentary; but in this case it is the upper half of the page which has been obliterated; we have, however, two or three complete sentences, which enable us, despite the absence of a date, to divine its relation to the preceding one. It is clear that Boswell had not heard of the death of Churchill, and that Wilkes, in replying to the letter we have tried to reconstruct above, spoke of it. It would appear that he used his grief as an excuse for declining Boswell's invitation; at any rate, there was some obstacle to their meeting, for the next letter reads:

. . . Churchill's death fills me with generous sympathy with you. Is it not well that you pause and reflect a little? Might we not have an interview and continue the conversation on the immateriality of the soul which you had with my countryman Baxter many years ago at Brussels?

To men of philosophical minds there are surely moments in which they set aside their nation, their . . .

The water has destroyed for ever James Boswell's fine sentiment on the death of Churchill; but the next sentences are a priceless revelation of his typical method of approach: —

John Wilkes, the fiery Whig, would despise this sentiment. John Wilkes the gay profligate, would laugh at it. But John Wilkes the philosopher will feel it and will love it.

You have no objection to sitting up a little late.   Perhaps you may come to me tonight.   I hope at any rate you will dine with me tomorrow.

James Boswell is not easily put down.   You may not care to revel with him, because your heart is heavy with grief; but surely, surely, you will wish to comfort yourself by discussing the immortality of the soul.   Let philosophy replace hilarity.   You once told Boswell of your conversation with Baxter years ago, at Spa, on this very theme.   Now is the time to continue it!   Surely it is well for us revellers to pause and reflect a little.   In any case, the important business is that James Boswell should get into the presence of Wilkes.— And so, indeed, he did, either at Turin or some more southerly town.

The next letter of Boswell's is dated March 2, and is written in Latin, from Baiæ.   The tone of it makes clear that cordial relations between the two are now permanently established.   Their intimacy has progressed to the use of nicknames: Wilkes, because of his disloyalty to his King, is "Brutus," and Boswell is the "avenger of Cæsar." There has been much political brawling (*jurgia*) between them, much fine talk about literature and about Wilkes's proposed edition, with notes, of the poems of Churchill, whose literary executor he was.   There has been also much "classical" con-

versation,— whence this Latin letter,— not to
mention much joviality over the wine-bottle. But,
best of all, Wilkes has promised to join Boswell in
Naples — so much had been extracted from him
at Rome, where the association, begun at Turin,
had been continued. And now Boswell, after a
long and jolting journey over the Appian Way,
has reached Naples, — "dead Parthenope's dear
tomb,"—and, for some reason, had gone on to Baiæ.

Cæsaris ultor Brutum in exilio salutat. Hesterna
nocte Parthenopen hanc attigi. Membra fere fractus
dura ista Appia, quamvis tardissimus et etiam quoda-
modo serpens processus sum.

Egregium sane tempus invenio Baiis ; cælum luridum,
precellam fortem, pluvium continuum. Tali tempore
non mirandum si Anglus antiquus fune se suspenderet ;
sed pauper Scotus, si victum tantum habet, omni
tempore contentus vivit.

Precor mihi scire facias quando consortio tuo frui
possim ; non interest quo præbente domum, nam apud
te vel apud me vinum et hilaritas crunt. Ne oblivis-
caris promissi quod mihi Romæ dedisti, nos multum
simul fore Napoli. Summam spero voluptatem legendo
notas tuas acres in poemata acria Churchilli, qui nunc
cum Juvenale est. Musis amicus politica jurgia tradam
ventis. Latinam linguam scribere haud assuetus,
tamen in hac regione classica experiri volui. Excuses
et valeas.

Die 2º Martii,
    Anno 1765.

Wilkes was already in Naples. He had had the same jolting in getting there that had almost demolished the limbs of Boswell. The pavement of the Appian Way, he tells his daughter, was "intolerably hard, and so slippery that the horses were continually coming down on their knees." There were bad holes even in the road from Capua to Naples. Wilkes's promise to be with Boswell was redeemed. Together they ascended Vesuvius. Although a "clear cold day," the sixteenth of March, was chosen for the expedition, they sacrificed their skin to the blazing sun and the burning heat of volcanic ashes. According to Wilkes's account, he, for his part, was pushed and pulled to the summit by the efforts of five men; nor can we believe that our friend Boswell, who was of no athletic frame and was given to self-indulgence, acquitted himself with more distinction. From Wilkes's vivid account of the crater, it is easy to imagine the pair of them, prone on their bellies and suffocated by the smoke, peering down the crater at the ragged mountains of yellow sulphur below. When the wind swept the smoke towards them, they were obliged "hastily to retire," and descended in great discomfort, almost up to the knees in ashes. Boswell never forgot this exploit, and decades later, when writing to Wilkes, referred to himself as "your Vesuvius fellow-traveller."

Such experiences, indeed, serve to draw men together; old associations of this kind are the best antidote to estrangement. James Boswell, by reason of his association with Wilkes in a foreign land, thus completed his conquest of the great man by establishing a common fund of memories on which they might draw in future. "The many pleasant hours which we passed together at Naples," wrote Boswell on his return, a month later, to Rome, "shall never be lost." — "I shall never forget your civilities to me," Wilkes had told the young man at parting. "You are engraven upon my heart."

Boswell and Wilkes did not meet again upon the Continent. The younger man returned to Rome, to resume his studies of antiquities; but he did not neglect the friendship which had been so happily begun. Wilkes had agreed to correspond with him, and Boswell was not the man to permit him to treat that promise lightly. He wrote Wilkes two long letters from Rome, and one from Terni. The contents of these letters afford us a notion of the kind of conversation that went on between the two, much of which was, plainly, political banter. Wilkes was amazed, and he was delighted — who can doubt it? — with the effrontery of a young man who dared to make him the subject of a satirical poem and to instruct him with regard to the amiable character of his ancient enemy, Lord Bute.

"Some days ago," he writes to Wilkes from Rome, "nothing would serve me but to write you an Heroic Epistle." Boswell was ever vaguely ambitious to produce satiric verse, and in the course of his life published a number of such pieces, besides leaving behind him a large quantity of verse in MS., apparently designed for publication. There is no doubt that he planned to print the "Epistle to Wilkes" if he could bring himself to finish it, not so much, perhaps, for its poetic value, as for indubitable evidence to the British public that he was now intimate with the notorious politician in exile. In a later letter he told Wilkes that he had had a flow of spirits, in which he had dashed off some hundred and fifty lines of the Epistle. It is to be hoped that this continuation was sprightlier than the following specimen, which he submitted to Wilkes : —

> To thee, gay Wilkes, tho' outlaw'd, still as gay,
> As when Dan Armstrong wrote his German "Day,"
> Another Scot now sends his English rhymes ;
> Spite of the Whiggish broils which mark our times ;
> Spite of the rude North-Briton's factious rage,
> And all th' abuse of thy imputed page.

Armstrong and Wilkes had once quarrelled over a poem of the former's, entitled "Day," which the

Scottish poet, then resident in Germany, had entrusted to Wilkes for publication, and in which Wilkes had ventured to make certain alterations. But there was no danger of a quarrel between the demagogue and his new poet. Wilkes chuckled at the lines, and told his young friend to go ahead with the verses. He was amused at Boswell's Toryism, and apparently enjoyed his invectives, which he deliberately elicited for the genial purpose of laughing at them.

"You may think as you please," Boswell writes, "but I have no small pride in being able to write to you with this gay good humour, for I do, in my conscience, believe you to be an enemy to the true old British Constitution, and to the order and happiness of society. That is to say, I believe you to be a very Whig and a very libertine."

When you are corresponding with an eccentric plain-dealer like this, you must give yourself over either to indignation or to amusement; the only alternative is to mend your ways. Wilkes, who was himself a plain-dealer, enjoyed this turning of the tables, and so the friendship continued.

But it was destined to be very seriously interrupted by the tour to Corsica. Letters, it is true, were exchanged between them after Boswell's return from the island. Wilkes wrote with true sympathy on the occasion of the death of Boswell's

mother, and Boswell invited Wilkes to visit him
at Auchinleck; but there was no real intimacy between them for many years afterwards.   This was
probably due in part to Boswell's growing friendship with Johnson. In the "Life," Boswell, speak-
ing of his return from the Continent, remarks: "I
having mentioned that I had passed some time with
Rousseau in his wild retreat, and having quoted
some remark made by Mr. Wilkes, with whom I
had spent many pleasant hours in Italy, Johnson said (sarcastically), 'It seems, Sir, you have
kept very good company abroad, Rousseau and
Wilkes!'" Boswell was not yet sufficiently sure of
himself and Johnson to propose bringing the two
together. And so they drifted apart.

In the year 1774, Wilkes's amazing political
fortunes elevated him to the office of Lord Mayor
of London. Boswell at once renewed the old
associations. He addressed him as "My Lord"
(to Wilkes's express disgust), and they were classical and gay, as in their Italian days. Wilkes gave
Boswell a special invitation to the great dinner
in the Mansion House on Easter Tuesday, 1775.
This entertainment, as was fitting when a popular
idol had become chief magistrate of the city, surpassed in magnificence all former events of the
sort. The press-cuttings preserved at the Guild-
hall give the following account of it: —

In the Egyptian Hall, where the company dined, was
a beautiful piece, painted in an inimitable taste, which,
it is said, represented the triumph of Bacchus and
Ariadne, or love united with wine.   Besides the usual
profusion of wines and eatables, which were remarkably
good in their kind, and set off in the greatest elegance,
as well as much warmer than commonly is the case at
those great dinners, the guests were here presented with
another novelty, which had a most pleasing effect,
many of Mr. Cox's pieces of mechanism, from the
Museum, all in full tune, and which continued their
musical movements, during the greatest part of the
dinner.   The dessert was in the same pleasing style, at
once great and elegant.   In the ball-room taste and
magnificence prevailed.

Among the "elegant and orderly company" is
found the name of Mr. Boswell, and, later, this
highly characteristic anecdote, which bears on its
face the marks of its authenticity: —

At dinner Mr. Boswell, who had taken care to secure
good room, seeing Mr. Colman in want of a place,
called to him, and gave him one beside himself, saying,
"See what it is to have a Scotchman for your friend at
Mr. Wilkes's table."   A little time after there came a
foreign waiter with something; Mr. Boswell talked to
him in German, upon which Mr. Colman wittily observed, "I have certainly mistaken the place to-day.   I
thought I was at the Mansion House, but I must surely
be at St. James's, for here are nothing but Germans
and Scots."

Boswell made the most of his new opportunities, promised Miss Wilkes (now the Lady Mayoress) a copy of the Glasgow edition of the poems of Gray, and the Lord Mayor a present of some black game, and, moreover, requested the renewal of their correspondence.

It is long since I enjoyed the pleasure of your correspondence. Will you renew it with me now? I should value, as curiosities of the first rate, lively sallies from a Lord Mayor of London, such as those from Mr. Wilkes which are preserved in my cabinet.

But no letters appear to have been written as a result of this request.

Boswell's most remarkable exploit with Wilkes occurred the next year: it consisted, as all the world knows, in bringing the demagogue and Dr. Johnson together at dinner at Mr. Dilly's. The success of this social experiment, which would have taxed the skill of the most accomplished dowager in London, was a source of permanent satisfaction to Boswell, who prefaces his description of it in the "Life" with the proud words, "Pars magna fui." The description constitutes perhaps the most famous page in that famous book. It has delighted the world of readers ever since; and that delight should be taken as a measure of the colour and excitement which James Boswell knew how to introduce into the conventional life in which he moved. He was an irritant in a group which is likely to move sluggishly, according to dull precedent, avoiding novelties and revisions of judgment.

Everybody, I repeat, knows the story of the Wilkes dinner, and many know the story of its successor, which occurred five years later at the same place; but what few people know is that Boswell proposed, and almost succeeded in bringing about, a third meeting. He was not the man to halt in the course that he was running. It was next his ambition to persuade Dr. Johnson to go to dinner at Wilkes's own house. To see Johnson under the roof of the man who had been his bitter antagonist — to bring Mercury and Ursa Major into conjunction — that would be a constellation worth observing! What a page for the "Life of Johnson"!

It is possible that the invitation which Wilkes issued to Johnson was the result of a jest or a wager. In May, 1783, Boswell undertook to negotiate for a dinner of his old friends, John and Charles Dilly, at the home of Wilkes. He did so in a highly characteristic epistle, in which he distributed titles with a free hand, complimented Miss Wilkes, reminded her father that, if he should ever become a widower, he might yet sue for her hand, and so become Wilkes's son-in-law, introduced the inevitable quotation from Horace and the equally

inevitable jest on Wilkes's ugly face.   It would be
difficult to find a more characteristic letter, yet it
covers barely a single page in Boswell's generous
hand.   It is necessary to add that the High Sheriff of Bedford is Mr. John Dilly, the Lord Chamberlain of London is Wilkes, and the Vesuvius
traveller, of course, Boswell himself.

GENERAL PAOLI'S
SOUTH AUDLEY STREET, 12 May.

DEAR SIR, —
   As I undertook to be the negociator of the dinner at
your house — the High Sheriff of Bedfordshire, his
brother Mr. Charles Dilly, and an old Vesuvius fellow-
traveller — I beg to know if next Sunday, the 18th will
be convenient for the Chamberlain of London.   This
is *omnia magna loquens.*   My best compliments to Miss
Wilkes.   She knows my conditional threatening that
you should have been *mon beau père.   Ah qu'il est beau!
Vale et me ama.*

JAMES BOSWELL.

At this dinner — if it took place as planned —
there were present three of the *principals* who had
appeared at the dinner when Johnson was first
presented to Wilkes, and it would be but natural
for the conversation to turn upon that event.   Be
this as it may, on the following Wednesday Boswell wrote to Wilkes: —

   Mr. Boswell finds that it would not be unpleasant
to Dr. Johnson to dine at Mr. Wilkes's.   The thing

would be so *curiously benignant,* it were a pity it should not take place. Nobody but Mr. Boswell should be asked to meet the Dr. Mr. Boswell goes for Scotland Friday the 30th. If then a card were sent to the Dr. for Monday, Tuesday, or Wednesday without delay, it is to be hoped he would be fixed, and notice will be sent to Mr. Boswell.

But Johnson, capricious as a prima donna (or an heiress in a post-chaise), changed his mind. He would not dine with Wilkes. He had engagements. In a curt note, "Mr. Johnson returns thanks to Mr. and Miss Wilkes for their kind invitation, but he is engaged for Tuesday to Sir Joshua Reynolds, and for Wednesday to Mr. Paradise," he put an end to the negotiations. This note was made the more insulting by being handed to Boswell for transmission to Wilkes. It is possible that Boswell had difficulty in obtaining even this formal word. There was almost certainly a scene. The "Life" is silent on the entire matter, and there is no entry for May 24, the date of Johnson's note. Those who, like Boswell, love the record of life as it actually passed, will regret his silence on this subject; but they will regret still more that the dinner in Wilkes's house did not occur. That loss is the world's.

Of Boswell's later relations with Wilkes there is but little to record. There are references to other dinners (after Johnson's death) at Dilly's and at Wilkes's house in Kensington Gore, where, no doubt, Boswell met Wilkes's mistress. The letters in reference to them have the same ring as the earliest ones, — "Pray let us meet oftener," — the same proposal that Wilkes should make an *amende honorable* to the Scots. There is, unhappily, a reference to money which Boswell has borrowed of Wilkes. And, last of all, six weeks after the appearance of the "Life of Johnson," when Wilkes was sixty-four years old, a note — indeed, a mere scrap — which well reveals Boswell's undying passion for written evidence, as well as his instinct for collecting.

June 25.

My dear Sir, —

You said to me yesterday of my *magnum opus*, "It is a wonderful book." Do confirm this to me, so as I may have your *testimonium* in my archives at Auchinleck. I trust we shall meet while you are in town.

Every most truly yours,

James Boswell.

The cabinet at Auchinleck! What would one not have given to inspect it? Within it were treasured the letters which Boswell had received from the Great — letters from Johnson, from Rousseau, from David Hume, from Paoli, from Burke, from Garrick, from Wilkes, and a thousand

others.   Moreover, there were deposited the notes
of his conversations and his manifold memorabilia
— a treasure of documents for the life of the times.
The collection must have been shown to many a
visitor to Auchinleck in the latter days; but literary visitors, alas, were few; and none has recorded any description of it.   When it perished,
there disappeared for ever materials out of which
Boswell, had he lived, might have woven the story
of his association with Wilkes.   Compared with
the "Life of Johnson" such a story would have
been a mere sketch; but it would have been a
sketch from a master-hand.   There would have
been in it, moreover, an *élan*, a hilarity, a love of
mischief and impudence, that could not, by the
nature of Boswell's relations with Johnson, appear
in the great "Life."   There would have been, in
short, more fun.   But, because Boswell was a
genius, there would have been something more —
a vivid characterisation of Wilkes, done by a man
who loved him but had no illusions about him, a
man who had penetrated into the inmost secrets
of his life, yet had remained unaffected by his
political views.   It might not have been a defini-
tive study of eighteenth-century radicalism, but it
would have been Wilkes.   His name would have
been in no danger of disappearing from the minds
of men.   The decree of fate (and Hogarth), by

which his demagogy has been subtly emphasised in
the minds and memories of men, might then have
been altered by the work of a greater artist than
Hogarth, and John Wilkes, the gay and fascinating
John Wilkes, might have been remembered for
something other than the evil that he did.

CHAPTER V

BOSWELL AND HIS ELDERS: LORD AUCHINLECK
SIR ALEXANDER DICK, GENERAL PAOLI

BOSWELL was one of those unusual young persons who deliberately and by preference seek out the companionship of men twice their age. His three most celebrated friends, Wilkes, General Paoli, and Samuel Johnson, were, respectively, thirteen, fifteen, and thirty-one years older than he. His two favourite friends in Scotland, Sir David Dalrymple (Lord Hailes) and Sir Alexander Dick, were, respectively, fourteen and thirty-seven years older than he. Association with younger men he found vivacious but profitless; their conversation was not such as a man would care to record. In his friendship with older men there was always an attempt to gain, as it were at second-hand, all the treasures of a long experience. When the atmosphere became too rarefied, he could always sink back again to the more primitive type of comradeship. In one of his early letters to Sir David, soon after the acquaintance with Johnson had begun, Boswell wrote: —

I must own to you that I have for some time past been in a miserable unsettled way, and been connected with people of shallow parts, altho' agreeably vivacious. But I find a flash of merriment a poor equivalent for internal comfort. I thank God that I have got acquainted with Mr. Johnson. He has done me infinite service. He has assisted me to obtain peace of mind.

We should all do well, I think, to rid our minds of the familiar conception of Boswell as lost in an ecstasy of hero-worship and breathless with adulation; and to think of him, rather, as getting from his association with his elders a double portion of life, enjoying the fruits of experience without sacrificing the avidity of youth. He was, as it were, buying experience in the cheapest market; and to him a full and rich experience of life was the *summum bonum.*

Because of this desire for a varied experience, he was ever, when with older men, putting himself in an attitude not so much of worship as of inquiry. What did the actual experience of life have to say in answer to the thousand questions that crowded his eager, restless mind? If his elders had attained serenity, it must have been by finding some answer to these thousand disturbing questions. If not, whence rose their peace of mind? Thus Boswell habitually teased Johnson on the subject of the freedom of the will, not, I think, because he conceived of him as a greater philosopher than any who had ever touched on the subject, but because, seeing Johnson's comparative mastery of the business of living, he was most desirous of knowing what solution of the problem had appealed to him as acceptable. If one could actually extract from association with his elders a body of philosophy, tested by personal experience and illustrated by personal anecdote, what an education it would be! He has himself made the matter clear, in his "Tour to Corsica": —

The contemplation of such a character [as Paoli], really existing, was of more service to me than all I had been able to draw from books, from conversation, or from the exertions of my own mind. I had often enough formed the idea of a man continually such as I could conceive in my best moments. But this idea appeared like the ideas we are taught in the schools to form of things which may exist, but do not; of seas of milk and ships of amber. But I saw my highest idea realised in Paoli. It was impossible for me, speculate as I pleased, to have a little opinion of human nature in him.

For this reason, again, he was perpetually seeking advice. Indeed, the seeking of advice became with Boswell, as it does with many of the young, what is euphemistically termed a "habit." Demanding advice of one's elders is not infrequently merely a means of calling attention to oneself. The seeker presents himself, alternately, in the actual and the ideal rôle, and his self-love is flat-

tered. If he succeeds in getting his advice, he has
succeeded in making himself an object of concern
to the elder generation. It is, in short, a harmless
kind of vanity. It will be recalled that Boswell pardoned the envoy at Berlin for not giving the advice
which he wanted, adding, "To enter into a detail of
the little circumstances which compose the felicity
of another is what a man of any genius can hardly
submit to." Nevertheless, it was such a compre-
hension as that which Boswell demanded and was
always hoping to get. On his own side, he had
much to offer in return. Sheer appreciation, for
example. Is not age for ever fretting because
youth will not listen to its counsels? Here was a
youth eager to listen. And then he could keep age
in touch with a younger generation, if age had
broadmindedness enough to let him upset its conservatism and introduce colour and movement
into life. One might tour the Seven Provinces,
or the farthest Hebrides, in company with youth;
one might dine with Jack Wilkes, or attempt to
scrape acquaintance with the King of Sweden.
Life is not over at sixty.

It is clear that this attitude is not merely filial,
dutiful, submissive. It is not the posture of obedient son in the presence of revered father. In a
word, it is not hero-worship. There is too much
in it of give-and-take, too much that originates

with the younger party to the contract. Of his
own father Boswell never succeeded in making a
companion. Perhaps he never tried. At any
rate, long before we know them with any degree
of intimacy, they had begun to draw apart; and it
is likely that the dissimilarity of their natures had
prevented them, from the beginning, from achiev-
ing any genuine intimacy or comradeship. Boswell always respected Lord Auchinleck, and in
those rare moments when his father gave him
plenty of rein, he loved him; but in general the
father was *dour*. He was totally unfitted to understand or make allowance for the tastes and habits
of his son James. By what jest of fate had he,
the hard-headed, sharp-tongued, contentious Calvinist judge, begotten this runagate? By what
methods could he hope to sober the creature and
fasten his ever wayward thoughts on the Scots law,
so that he might rise in time to the bench, as his
father had done, and reign worthily over Auchinleck? But it was of no use. "Jamie" had gone
"clean gyte." How could the thrifty father be
expected to realise that his son's love of social life
would ever be of more worth to the world than the
earnest application to duty of the most industrious
apprentice that ever lived?

As for "Jamie," his instinctive affection was
gradually extinguished by the father's upbraiding.

Constant fretting at the young will in time wear away all affection; confidence and mutual respect disappear long before. "My lord," said the son, "was solid and composed, Boswell was light and restless." The younger man felt that he was treated like a boy (as, no doubt, he was); and even after he was married and independent, he was fain to consume a large amount of strong beer in order to get through the ordeal of a visit in his father's home — all of which could not have tended to allay the ever-rising hostility between them.

They differed sharply over the entail of the estate of Auchinleck, Boswell wishing to confine the succession to the male heirs. The question was of no practical importance, for there was no lack of male heirs; but it none the less increased the friction between them. They were better off when they were far apart. A visit to London meant to Boswell, among other things, escape from a carping father.

And yet the father made a distinct appeal to the son. He had lost his son's heart, but fascinated his creative imagination. Boswell never ceased to realise that Lord Auchinleck was remarkably good "material." To adopt the phraseology of a later century, the old gentleman "belonged in a novel." His keen wits and his strong national prejudices flowered naturally into racy humour;

he was chock-full of anecdote; although a judge and an aristocrat, he had the vivid speech and the shrewd observation of a man who has learned from Nature and not from books. But Lord Auchinleck, though a highly-educated man and a devoted, if not pedantic, student of the classics, had never lost his mother wit. One thing at least James Boswell inherited from his father, his love of a good story. He filled the pages of his Commonplace Book with his father's vivacious anecdotes, and in so doing produced the best possible portrait of him. It is odd that such perfect artistic sympathy should exhibit itself after the decay of all filial devotion. It is the triumph of art over discord.

Of certain of James's associates the old gentleman did not disapprove. He liked Sir David, and listened to his intercessions on the son's behalf. He approved of Sir Alexander Dick. Neither of these gentlemen would take James far from home or distract his attention from the charms of the Scots law. Sir Alexander, in particular, was a safe associate. He was, to be sure, thirty-seven years older than James, but James had a fondness for older men, and a "way" with them, if only they would give him a chance.

Sir Alexander was now the head of the Dick family and residing at Prestonfield, or Priestfield

Parks, the family estate at the foot of Arthur's
Seat, near Edinburgh. He was a man of classical
learning, who liked to fancy that there was something Horatian in his peaceful retirement into rural
life. He wrote verses and cultivated the soil, in
imitation of Vergil's "Georgics," and threw open
his hospitable doors to all comers. He told Boswell
that he remembered to have had a thousand people
in a year to dine at his house. He was a gracious
gentleman, who loved men of genius, and was glad
to cultivate the acquaintance of any who might be
near Edinburgh. Allan Ramsay and David Hume
were his intimate friends; the Bishop of London,
Alexander Pope, and Benjamin Franklin were
among his acquaintances. Franklin, with his son,
visited Prestonfield, probably in the year 1759,
lingered there some days, and on his return to England, wrote a poem, beginning, "Joys of Prestonfield, adieu," in which he praised the "beds that
never bugs molest." Sir Alexander's table fairly
groaned with food. He once wrote in his diary:[1]
"Willie's birthday. Mr. James Boswell and the
India Mr. Boswell, Mrs. Young, etc., etc., all dined
here, and Mr. Mercer, and danced. We had a fine
piece of boiled beef and greens, a large turkey, some
fine chickens, 250 fine asparagus from my hot bed,

[1] January 7, 1777. Lady Forbes's *Curiosities of a Scots
Charta Chest*, p. 257.

and a fine pig, — all from the farm and wine from the farm (i.e., curran and gooseberry) and Greek from the Consul of Leghorn, and claret and port and punch and a fine Parmesan cheese, also from Leghorn." It is easy to understand why Boswell found in Prestonfield the best possible substitute for the social joys of London.

When Boswell went to Italy in the spring of 1765, Sir Alexander interested himself greatly in the trip. He had himself travelled in Holland and Italy as a young man, and still had old acquaintances there who could be of service to Boswell. On Christmas Eve, 1764, Boswell wrote to him from Geneva a letter asking for introductions to Italian men of learning : —

My plan [he wrote] is to employ my whole time in the study of antiquitys and the fine arts, for which I shall have such noble opportunitys that I hope to form a taste which may contribute to my happiness as long as I live. . . . I know no man more capable and who will be more ready to assist me than you, Sir.

The letter is particularly valuable because in it Boswell announces the route which he intends to follow through Italy. His plan was to cross from Milan to Venice, then to visit Rome and Naples, and afterwards to go to Florence and Genoa. As a matter of fact, he seems to have postponed the

visit to Venice till after he had been to Rome and
Naples — a change of plan which was undoubtedly
due to a desire to keep close to Wilkes, whom he
had met in Turin.   However, when this letter was
written, Wilkes was not yet on the horizon; Boswell was still cultivating Rousseau, but he was
anxious to provide for the associations of the future. "You will oblige me greatly," he continues,
"if you will recommend me as your friend to some
learned and ingenious men from whom I may receive instruction, and may catch the exquisite
enthusiasm of true taste.   When I come home to
Scotland, I shall endeavour to make you some return by my conversation at your classical villa of
Prestonfield."

Sir Alexander did as he was requested, and gave
Boswell an introduction to Camillo Paderni, the
Italian scholar and antiquary, who was among the
earliest explorers of Herculaneum, and was now in
charge of all the antiquities unearthed in the dis-
trict.   Under his personal escort, Boswell visited
the ruins.   After his return to Rome in May, he
sent the following description of the visit to Sir
Alexander: —

Camillo shewed me the rich store of antiquitys which
have been found at Herculaneum. He has arranged
them with great judgment and taste. They fully answered my expectations. I had not only an oppor-

tunity of admiring the noble remains of sculpture and painting, but viewed with curious satisfaction the immense variety of every thing for the use of life which, as you well say, fairly brings back old time, as it were, face to face. One sees by this collection how far the ancients had carried every article of convenience, and how very similar their ordinary course of living has been to that of modern times. I shall not pretend to give you a detail of what I saw at Herculaneum, or to enter into a discussion of any particulars till I have the pleasure of being with you, when we can talk it over fully. I need not tell you how much I was charmed with the delightfull situation of Naples and with its classical environs. I past three weeks there, and employed my time to very good purpose. Upon my return to Rome, I engaged an antiquary, and went through what is called a course of antiquitys, which includes also the pictures. I have viewed the noble remains of Roman grandeur with venerable enthusiasm, and have seen most of the best churches and palaces in Rome. I regret, indeed, that my time here is so short, that I can have little more than the immediate pleasure of seeing the many fine things. To study them and to form a correct taste would keep me from home much longer than my father's inclination and my serious dutys can allow. I have as much feeling as any man, and from the remembrance of the treasures of Italy, joined to what I have yet to see, I doubt not to retain so much taste as never to be idle for want of elegant occupation. I must own I have been a little dissappointed in Italy. You know what divine ideas we form of it, and you know that it does not come up to them in several respects.   However, I shall certainly say, *meminisse juvabit*.

This is, I think, the longest description which Boswell ever wrote of those "sights" which are commonly supposed to absorb all the attention of tourists; and it is to be feared that the whole account was written with a view to pleasing Sir Alexander (whose classical enthusiasm was great) rather than to expressing actual preferences.   "I must own I have been a little dissappointed in Italy."   At the moment when Boswell wrote that sentence, he was out of touch with the Great.   He had left Wilkes a month before in Naples.   Months were yet to pass before he met Paoli.   He was compelled to content himself with the companionship of young Lord Mountstuart (afterwards fourth Earl of Bute), who was making the Grand Tour in company with a tutor.   Boswell and he travelled together for a time, journeying northwards from Rome.[1]   There was genuine affection between the two of them, but nevertheless Lord Mountstuart was young — younger, indeed, by four years — and Boswell felt the difference in the quality of the association.   The viscount showed him the letters of his father, Lord Bute, and Boswell made what he could out of this association at second-hand.   He

[1] When, a year or so later, Boswell was admitted to the bar, he dedicated his thesis for admission to the young viscount.

had, at any rate, the pleasure of writing to Wilkes that that demagogue had been unfair to Lord Bute.

It was probably in Rome that Boswell met a gentleman by the name of John Dick, cousin to Sir Alexander, who was the British Consul at Leghorn. In the course of discussing with him his relation to Sir Alexander, Boswell stumbled upon a most interesting discovery, fraught with pleasant consequences for all concerned. This was no less than the fact that Consul Dick was a baronet in his own right — a fact of which he had remained hitherto in complete ignorance. But Boswell, who had interested himself in Sir Alexander Dick as a possible subject for a biography, was acquainted with the details of the family history, and was therefore able to tell Consul Dick facts about his own descent of which he himself was ignorant. The founder of the line had been a Sir William Dick, the first baronet, who had advanced money to King Charles I, had become impoverished during the Civil Wars, and had died bankrupt. His sons scattered, and trace of the male heir was lost, the title descending through a *daughter*, to whom a new patent of baronetcy was issued, with remainder to her heirs male. Of this title Sir Alexander Dick was now the heir. But the *direct* male descendant of the first Sir William was the consul. This discovery Boswell communicated, not only to

Consul Dick, but, later, to Sir Alexander Dick, who had among the family papers, as Boswell knew, information regarding the first baronet.

This whole incident delighted the feudal soul of our hero, and on his return to Scotland he at once busied himself to prove the succession which he had discovered. It was a long process; but at last, in March, 1768, John Dick was "served heir" to his great-great-grandfather, the first baronet, and Boswell carried the proofs up to London, together with a *retour*, or official extract of the verdict of the jury who heard the proof. Boswell's account of the incident, in a letter to Sir Alexander, is as follows : —

On my arrival in London, I put up at the Star and Garter in Bond Street, and who do you think happened to be in that very house, at a club, but our excellent friend, the Consul? I went to him. He immediately came to me. We embraced, and I told him in a hurry all the principal circumstances of what had been done in Scotland. In the evening I waited upon him to supper and was rejoiced at seeing again *La Signora Consolessa*[1] of whom you have heard so much, and have formed a very just idea.

I was a great man, for I came laden with valuable things. I produced the *retour*, which I read in English, with an audible voice. I then displayed the magnificent Burgess ticket, which was very much admired, and

[1] Lady Dick.

I give you my word that my heart beat with real gladness as I read it also aloud. I next displayed the portrait of the venerable Sir William, and then the worthy baronet's letter made the *bonne bouche*. You may figure me quite at home, and in high spirits investing your cousins with their titles! "Sir John Dick, my service to you; Lady Dick, I have the honour to drink your Ladyship's good health." So it went, and I know not when I was happier. . . .

What do you think of my Lady Dick's bounty to me? She has this morning made me a present of the most elegant sword I ever saw — steel, richly carved and embossed, and gilt; in short, quite the princely sword for the Laird of Auchinleck. It will delight you to see it when we meet. I will come and strut at Prestonfield.

The story is continued in the same tone, a week later : —

I think now our worthy friend will be completely fixed in his dignity. He was presented to the King as knight . . . and both he and Lady Dick have kist hands, and are universally acknowledged. I never rested until I had the brass plate on his door changed and ornamented with "Sir John Dick."

Boswell's exertions on behalf of Sir John not only brought him a new friend, but also deepened the affection between him and Sir Alexander, who now had a new realisation of his abilities. The proposal to "Boswellise" Sir Alexander was for a time taken very seriously, both by the biographer

and the subject. In 1777, Sir Alexander wrote in
his diary: "Last week Mr. James Boswell, my
friend, expressed a desire to make a biographical
account of my life to my 74th year. . . . I looked
over many jottings and [records] of past times, and
we had some droll interviews, and it becomes, he
says, very interesting." Sir Alexander turned over
a bundle of these papers to Boswell, who appears
actually to have begun the composition of the
work, for, in October, 1778, he refers definitely to
the existence of a "biography." In a letter of this
date, Boswell, after commending Sir Alexander for
the account which he has given of the "public exertions" of his life, now demands a more intimate
kind of information.

Mark your agreeable freinds with whom you have
corresponded, and refer to the treasure of letters which
I hope to assist in arranging. I could wish, too, that
you would mark your *studies*, and as far as you please
your *opinions* in religion and politicks. I value very
highly the confidence you put in me. . . . Your *opinions*, I suppose, you will mark with your own hand.
For though I beleive them to be truly pious, yet there
may be a *liberality* in them which may be misunder-
stood by your secretary. You are an *elder*, and, I
trust, a brother Christian.

It would seem, from this extract, as if Boswell,
having wearied of his biographical task, had now

turned it over to Sir Alexander to complete, with the assistance of his daughter and secretary, Miss Jessy Dick. If such be the case, there is nothing surprising in it, for Boswell, by this time (1778), was already absorbed in his Johnsonian plans, and had no time for lesser game.

But there was no interruption of the pleasant relations with Sir Alexander Dick. He lived to the advanced age of eighty-two. He had known Boswell from boyhood, and throughout their long association there had never occurred, so far as we know, anything to spoil the pleasure and mutual respect which they felt for each other. There was nothing startling or romantic in their friendship, for it was of the ordinary, enduring kind which, by reason of its very simplicity, is all the more valuable to us as revealing a side of Boswell's character which is generally neglected.

A more distinguished but no less devoted friend than Sir Alexander was Pasquale Paoli, the great Corsican patriot. In his relations with Paoli there mingled an element of romantic adventure which was entirely lacking in the other friendships of Boswell's life. For Paoli he felt a reverence that he did not display even toward Johnson, since he saw in his career—as indeed did all Europe—an attempt to vindicate the essential dignity of man-

kind. Out of a group of half-barbarous islanders
he had undertaken to make a nation imbued with
the sacred principles of liberty and equality. He
was a modern Æneas. The eyes of "republicans"
everywhere were turned towards Paoli. The name
of a flourishing town in Pennsylvania perpetuates
the interest which was felt in Paoli and the Corsicans by the people of America. Rousseau was to
be the law-giver of the new nation. "Come back
twenty or thirty years hence," said Paoli to Boswell, "and we'll shew you arts and sciences." *Ars
longa.*

In young, aspiring, or liberty-loving nations
Boswell was always interested. He was, from the
first, an American sympathiser. He had strange
notions about the rights of Ireland. Although a
Lowlander, he had a passionate devotion to the
clannish life of the Highlands, and loved to assume
the style of an "old lord of Scotland." He therefore became deeply interested in the Corsicans, of
whom he had heard much from the Earl Marischal
and from Rousseau. He determined to go and see
for himself the heroic nation in the infant stages
of its history, and to know and converse with this
maker of nations. It was easy to persuade the
emotional Rousseau to give him the necessary introduction to Paoli. The difficult thing was to
escape being shot for a spy.

There exist two accounts of Boswell's first
meeting with Paoli, which are so neatly supplementary that it seems strange that they should
never before have been set down side by side, for
it is seldom that so interesting a meeting has
been described by both the "principals." Boswell
himself wrote the following account of it in his
"Tour to Corsica" : —

He asked me what were my commands for him. I
presented him a letter from Count Rivarola,[1] and when
he had read it, I shewed him my letter from Rousseau.
He was polite, but very reserved. I had stood in the
presence of many a prince, but I never had such a trial
as in the presence of Paoli. I have already said that
he is a great physiognomist. In consequence of his
being in continual danger from treachery and assassina-
tion, he has formed a habit of studiously observing
every new face. For ten minutes we walked backwards
and forwards through the room, hardly saying a word,
while he looked at me, with a steadfast, keen, and pene-
trating eye, as if he searched my very soul.

This interview was for a while very severe upon me.
I was much relieved when his reserve wore off, and he
began to speak more. I then ventured to address him
with this compliment to the Corsicans, "Sir, I am upon
my travels, and have lately visited Rome. I am come
from seeing the ruins of one brave and free people : I
now see the rise of another."

He received my compliment very graciously.

[1] The Sardinian Consul at Leghorn.

" Bozzy "

Engraving by F. Holl, from a sketch by Sir Thomas Lawrence

Some years later the incident was recalled by Paoli when he was visiting the Thrales at Streatham, and he gave Fanny Burney the following account, which she records in her "Diary": —

"He came," he said, "to my country, and he fetched me some letter of recommending him; but I was of the belief he might be an impostor and an espy; for I look away from him, and in a moment I look to him again, and I behold his tablets. Oh! he was to the work of writing down all I say! Indeed, I was angry. But soon I discover he was no impostor and no espy; and I only find I was myself the monster he had come to discern. Oh, [Boswell] is a very good man; I love him indeed; so cheerful! so gay! so pleasant! but at the first, oh! I was indeed angry."

The intimacy which grew up between the two men was destined, before many years had passed, to be renewed. "Remember that I am your friend, and write to me," Paoli had said to Boswell as he left him; but he could hardly have conceived how deep and true that friendship was to become, or how serviceable to him and the cause which he represented the young Scotsman might be. The "Tour to Corsica," to which Boswell added as a supplementary title, "Memoirs of Paoli," has been a delightful book to generations of readers, but its political significance and its practical value as Corsican "propaganda" have been forgotten.

Boswell was almost the first British visitor to the island. "Tell them what you have seen here," Paoli said, when Boswell asked him what service he could render the cause after returning to England. "They will be curious to ask you. A man come from Corsica will be like a man come from the Antipodes." And so indeed he was.

Sir George Otto Trevelyan, whose authority no one is likely to impugn, after remarking that Boswell wrote "what is still by far the best account of the island that has ever yet been published," goes on to speak of his influence in the following way : —

How real was the effect produced by Boswell's narrative upon the opinion of his countrymen may be gathered from the unwilling testimony of those who regretted its influence, and thought little of its author. "Foolish as we are," wrote Lord Holland, "we cannot be so foolish as to go to war because Mr. Boswell has been in Corsica; and yet, believe me, no better reason can be given for siding with the vile inhabitants of one of the vilest islands of the world, who are not less free than all the rest of their neighbours, and whose island will enable the French to do no more harm than they may do us at any time from Toulon." Horace Walpole credited Boswell with having procured Paoli his pension of a thousand a year from the British Exchequer.[1]

Besides publishing the "Tour," in which the first genuine information about the personality of

[1] *Early History of Charles James Fox*, p. 135.

Paoli was given to the world, Boswell conceived the plan of soliciting articles on Corsica from his friends and acquaintances, and issuing a volume on behalf of the islanders. "British Essays in favour of the Brave Corsicans" appeared in 1769, the very year of Paoli's defeat by the French, to whom the Genoese had finally sold the storm-vexed island. In September of this year, Paoli landed in England. Walpole, who hated Paoli and Boswell (and, indeed, almost everyone else), wrote in his "Memoirs of the Reign of George III," "Paoli's character had been so advantageously exaggerated by Mr. Boswell's enthusiastic and entertaining account of him that the Opposition were ready to incorporate him in the list of popular tribunes." In that same category Walpole, too, had been willing to place him until he had the audacity to fight against the French. From that time on he became to Walpole a contemptible person, worthy of no better epithets than an "unheroic fugitive" and a "dirty fellow."

Paoli's reception in England, whither he fled after his defeat, was, however, flattering in the extreme. Boswell's account of it (here printed for the first time) is found in a letter to Sir Alexander Dick : —

Our illustrious chief has been received here with the greatest honour. The King desired to see him pri-

BRITISH ESSAYS

IN FAVOUR OF THE

BRAVE CORSICANS:

BY

SEVERAL HANDS.

COLLECTED AND PUBLISHED

By JAMES BOSWELL, Esq:

In medium mors omnis abit, perit obruta virtus.
Nos in conspicua sociis, hostique carina
Constituere Dei, Præbebunt æquora testes,
Præbebunt terræ, summis dabit insula saxis.
LUCAN.

LONDON:

PRINTED FOR EDWARD AND CHARLES DILLY,

IN THE POULTRY.

MDCCLXIX.

vately at the Queen's palace, where he went accordingly, and was a long time alone with his Majesty, who expressed himself in the most agreable manner as to Corsica.

I must tell you an anecdote which you will like. The King said, "I have read Boswell's book, which is well written [*scritto con spirito*]. May I depend upon it as an authentic account?" The General answered, "Your Majesty may be assured that every thing in that book is true, except the compliments which Mr. Boswell has been pleased to pay to his friend."

As for the later relations of Boswell and Paoli, are they not written in the "Life of Johnson"? If there be truth in that record, Paoli's affection for his eccentric young friend never wavered; it was apparently never necessary for Boswell to humour Paoli, and there were no storms of passion to endure, such as mark the more famous association of Boswell's life. For many years — until, indeed, Boswell came to reside in London in 1786 — General Paoli's house in South Audley Street was his headquarters during his London holiday. And who can doubt that, despite repeated fits of gloom, his presence there was grateful; for he came always as a harbinger of social joys, a bringer of new things, a perpetual enemy of inertia and sameness. To the sons and daughters of respectability his presence was no doubt an offence; but to his friends, who had learned to love him for his very oddities, his presence was a promise of gaiety and social converse, the very "nights and suppers of the gods" once more, brightening the workaday world.

CHAPTER VI

IN LOVE

Perhaps in Vanity Fair there are no better satires than letters . . . Vows, love, promises, confidences, gratitude, how queerly they read after a while! There ought to be a law in Vanity Fair ordering the destruction of every written document (except receipted tradesmen's bills) after a certain brief and proper interval. — Thackeray.

In all the varied business of living there is perhaps no matter which must be conducted more strictly according to rule and precedent than the business of wooing a wife. There is a recognised way of getting the thing accomplished (based, no doubt, on the instinct and experience of the race), and brave is the man who dares to adopt any other. "All the world loves a lover" — if he observes the conventions of the game; but if he does not, the world pours out upon the unfortunate creature the contempt which it always feels for those who do not accept its own methods.

One of these is furtiveness. There must be something clandestine about the first stages, if not all stages, of the process. Courtship is a kind of theft, and the amorous pair continue the policy of stealth long after their secret is known to the world. Indeed, the public demands it. If you feel the impulse to tell the story of your passion to a friend at Piccadilly Circus, you must refrain, even though he be the friend of your bosom. If you desire to print the verses which you have addressed to the lady of your choice, you must remind yourself that it is not done. Let the verses be discovered in the secret drawer of the escritoire after your death, and the public will be glad to read them.

Again, you must not seek advice. You may have the counsels of the world on every subject but this; but unless you are willing to be dubbed a fool, you must go unaided to meet this most momentous issue of life. Your friends, to be sure, will be the first to criticise you for not having somehow divined (and followed) the advice which they could not and would not give; but to this criticism you must be deaf. It is true that, if you care at all for your friends, the introduction of a new person into your old relationships may have consequences of the gravest importance; but to all these you must be blind.

Finally, you must be sure of yourself: you are not permitted to be in doubt whether or not the emotions you are experiencing may be true love or not. You may be wrong, but you must not doubt. If you finally wake to the realisation that you are, and have been, wrong, you may try again; but again you are not permitted to waver. You may perhaps be of so happy a temperament that a thousand ladies seem to you worthy of your love and capable of making you happy; but this view you must conceal as a heresy. The prize which you draw must make all other drawings seem blank; you must not scan and compare the blessings of other men. You may let men know of your disillusion or (ultimately) of your success, but you must not tell the story of your doubt, as you must not tell the story of your progress to success.

It has been necessary to analyse these rules because in the love-story that is to follow every one of them was outraged, and outraged repeatedly. To many the story will seem so preposterous as to be incredible. Let such readers recall their own life-long observance of the conventions of society, and get such satisfaction as they may out of the thought that they are not as James Boswell. Yet Boswell was a human being, who, after his strange wooings, became a loving husband.

Let the reader remember that the evidence which is to be placed before him is, in general, taken from letters written to the best loved of all his friends, the Reverend William Temple, the friend of his boyhood, his devoted correspondent and confidant. All his days Boswell felt a consuming desire to impart his emotions to a confidant, a desire worthy of comparison, perhaps, with that of the heroines in Racine's tragedies, save that it dispenses with the trappings of dignity and reserve, unwillingly abandoned, which distinguish the amorous ladies of the classical drama.   There was much to tell, and he could but rejoice that he had a friend to tell it to.   The story had begun in their boyhood, when the two foolish youngsters told each other of the kind of woman they would, in future, be willing to marry.

James, it would appear, pretended, in the beginning, to be mature and philosophical about it all. His ambitions, from the earliest moment, seem to have been astir, but they prompted him to dreams of greatness in the world of *men*. With the fulfillment of this dream, might not woman interfere? Long before they come within our ken, Temple and Boswell, or rather, Willie and James, had made a jest out of this dream of greatness, and they never forgot it as long as they lived.   Exactly what it signified to them we do not know, — for who shall interpret the cryptic wit of friendship? — but its general meaning is clear.   From the beginning Boswell had determined to be great, and from the beginning his ambition had been the subject of playful jest, such as friend uses with friend.   Again and again Boswell writes to Temple of some recent experience, "I was the Great Man."   With this dream of greatness there mingled thoughts of a helpmate who should be a worthy mistress of Auchinleck. Manifold were the natural graces and the endowments of fortune with which this lady must be blessed: wealth, beauty, and affability should unite their charms in the perfect harmony that was to make up this impossible she. As Shelley, in a later age, was always imagining that he had found at last his ideal embodied in the flesh, so, though in less exalted strains and with more earthly attributes, did our young Boswell dream that he had found his mate. In the first of his letters that has come down to us, we find this passage:—

You know I gave you a hint in my last of the continuance of my passion for Miss W——t; I assure you, I am excessively fond of her, so (as I have given you fair warning) don't be surprised if your grave, sedate, philosophick friend, who used to carry it so high, and talk with such a composed indifference of the beauteous sex, and whom you used to admonish not to turn an Old Man too soon, don't be thunderstruck, if this same fellow should all at once, *subito furore abreptus*, commence Don Quixote for his adorable Dulcinea. But to talk seriously, I at first fell violently in love with her, and thought I should be quite miserable if I did not obtain her; but now it is changed to a rational esteem of her good qualities, so that I should be extremely happy to pass my life with her, but if she does not incline to it,

I can bear it *æquo animo* and retire into the calm regions of Philosophy. She is, indeed, extremely pretty, and posest of every amiable qualification. She dances, sings, and plays upon several instruments equally well, draws with a great deal of taste, and reads the best authors; at the same time she has a just regard to true piety and religion, and behaves in the most easy, affable way. She is just such a young lady as I could wish for the partner of my soul, and you know that is not every one, for you and I have often talked how nice we would be in such a choice. I own I can have but little hopes, as she is a fortune of 30,000 pounds. Heaven knows that sordid motive is farthest from my thoughts. She invited me to come and wait upon her, so I went last week and drank tea; I was kindly entertained, and desired to come when convenient. I have reason to believe she has a very good opinion of me, and, indeed, a youth of my turn has a better chance to gain the affections of a lady of her character, than of any other; but (as I told you before) my mind is in such an agreable situation that being refused would not be so fatal as to drive me to despair, as your hot-brained, romantick lovers talk. Now, my dear friend, I sincerely ask ten thousand pardons for giving you the trouble of this long narration; but as it is a thing that concerns me a good deal, I could not but communicate it to you, and I know, when I inform you how happy it makes me to open my mind, you will forgive me. Pray never speak of it; you are the only person knows of it, except Mr. Love, who reads to her, and takes every unsuspected method to lend me his friendly assistance. Oh Willie! how happy should I be if she consented, some years after this, to make me blest! How transporting to think of such a lady to entertain you at Auchinleck!

Mr. Love, who was acting as the go-between and from whom the young man had probably first learned of his charmer, was the actor, whose acquaintance we made in a former chapter, and who eked out a precarious living by teaching elocution and borrowing money from Boswell. His efforts at match-making, however, were unsuccessful. The fair Miss W——t remains unidentified — the blanks which conceal her name are found in the manuscript — and disappears for ever from our story. She was not destined to become mistress of Auchinleck or to settle her £30,000 on our hero.

The letter from which the quotation is drawn is one written by Boswell before he was eighteen years old; he had yet to visit London, to complete his legal studies, and to make the Grand Tour. But even amid the distractions of London and foreign travel, his thoughts ran continually upon love. The search for his Dulcinea was to share in his search for the Great, and the problem was to be laid before more than one of his heroes.

Mention has already been made of a Baron de Zuylen whom Boswell met at Utrecht. His daughter Belle (or Isabella), who preferred the fanciful name, Zélide, which she had fabricated for herself, was exactly of Boswell's age, and like him in many respects. She was a true and very delightful daughter of the eighteenth century, vivacious in the extreme, yet subject to continual fits of sensibility, romantic yearnings, and dreams of free love. As a keen student of mathematics, — she rose early in the morning to master conic sections, — she soon emancipated herself from the Christian religion, which was not sufficiently exact to commend itself to her intelligence, and lost herself in the perplexities of metaphysical speculation. She longed to become rational in thought and conduct. But, with all the instincts of a bluestocking, she retained a pardonable vanity, and loved laughter and high spirits. In introspective fashion she wrote a "portrait" of herself, which is perhaps the best introduction to her somewhat complicated personality. It is in French and may be rendered as follows: —

Compassionate in temper, liberal and generous by inclination, Zélide is good only by principle; when she is sweet and yielding, give her credit for making an effort. When she is long civil and polite with people for whom she does not care, redouble your esteem, for it is martyrdom. Vain by nature, her vanity is boundless; knowledge and contempt of human kind had long since given her that. It goes, however, further even than that, as Zélide herself must admit. She thinks

Isabella de Zuylen, later Madame de Charriere

The " Zélide " of Boswell's romantic interlude at Utrecht

After a pastel by La Tour, 1766

already that glory is naught in comparison with happiness, and yet she would go far for glory.

At what period do the lights of the spirit take command of the inclinations of the heart? At that period will Zélide cease to be a coquette. Sad contradiction! Zélide, who would not wish to strike a dog unthinkingly or to crush a miserable insect, is perhaps willing, at certain moments, to make a man wretched — and this by way of amusing herself, in order to win a kind of glory which does not even flatter her reason and touches her vanity for but an instant. But the fascination is short; apparent success brings her back to herself; she no sooner realises her intention than she despises it, abhors it, and would fain renounce it for ever.

You ask me if Zélide is beautiful, pretty, or passable? I am not sure; it depends on whether she is loved or wishes to make herself loved. She has a fine throat, she is sure, and makes a little too much of it, at the expense of modesty. Her hand is not white, as she also knows, and she makes a jest of it, but she would prefer not to have to make it a subject of jest.

Tender in the extreme, and no less delicate, she can be happy neither with love nor without it. Friendship never had a holier or worthier temple than Zélide. Realising that she is too sensitive to be happy, she has almost ceased aspiring to happiness; she devotes herself to virtue, flees repentance, and seeks amusements. Pleasures are rare with her, but lively; she seizes them, and relishes them ardently. Knowing that plans are vain and the future uncertain, she is particularly desirous of rendering the moment happy as it flies.

Do you not guess it? Zélide is a little voluptuous;

her imagination can make her smile, even when her heart is heavy. Feelings too strong and lively for her mechanism, excessive activity, which lacks a satisfactory object — these are the source of all her ills. With organs less sensitive, Zélide would have had the soul of a great man; with less wit and sense, she would have been only a feeble woman.

This self-conscious, ambitious young lady and our self-conscious, ambitious young hero immediately became fast friends. They exchanged news of their melancholy symptoms, and Zélide listened with patience, and apparently with appreciation, to James's eternal advice. Then they would suddenly become hilarious, and the wit, as Boswell afterwards described it, flashed like lightning.

But Zélide's skepticism dismayed Boswell. Why should the mind of a young lady be possessed by the seven devils of rationalism? It is natural enough for a man to fall a victim; but females should not know that rationalism exists. Moreover, Boswell had himself been grounded in the principles of Christianity by Samuel Johnson, and was now reasonably sure of his faith. This was perhaps the most serious obstacle to their union, and Boswell set himself to remove it. But Zélide was not easily influenced, — had she not studied conic sections? — and so Boswell came to feel that perhaps, after all, Zélide was not the bride for him.

The Biographer in Meditation

Engraving by W. T. Green, from a sketch by George Langton

It would have been a comparatively simple thing to win her, had he set about it in a determined way, inasmuch as her parents liked the young man and encouraged his advances. "Il est fort mon ami," wrote Zélide, "et fort estimé de mon père et de ma mère, de sorte qu'il est toujours bien reçu quand il vient me voir." That he approached the subject a score of times, no one who reads the following letter can doubt. The pair of them seem to have reached a friendly conclusion that they were not suited for each other. He appears, with his infinite *naïveté*, to have explained her deficiencies to her; for once, when reckoning up her various lovers, she wrote, "Boswell will never marry me; if he did marry me, he would have a thousand regrets, for he is convinced that I would not suit him, and I do not know that I should care to live in Scotland." They agreed, therefore; and yet there was a magnetic force that drew them ever to each other. Boswell would make love to her, in spite of the finest assertions that he was not going to — that he was now a completely rational being, a philosophic creature, and what not. Perhaps in it all there mingled some misgivings at the thought of confessing to his father that he was desirous of bringing home a Dutch bride.

The letter which Boswell addressed to Zélide a

month or so after leaving Utrecht is the only love-
letter of his which has been preserved to us.   It is
also one of the longest that he ever wrote — so
long, indeed, that it is inadvisable to print it all.   I
excerpt those passages of it which deal with love.
It is to be hoped that the reader will not be deceived by the calmness and impudence of the
opening passages, but will note the crescendo of
feeling which culminates in the final postscript.

Consider, my dear Zélide, your many *real* advantages.
You are a daughter of one of the first familys in the
Seven Provinces; you have a number of relations of
rank.   You have a very handsom fortune, and I must
tell you, too, that Zélide herself is handsom.   You
have a title to expect a distinguished marriage.   You
may support a respected and an amiable character in
life.   Your genius and your many accomplishments
may do you great honour.   But take care.   If those
enchanting qualitys are not governed by Prudence,
they may do you a great deal of harm.   You have con-
fest to me that you are subject to hypochondria.   I
well beleive it.   You have a delicate constitution and a
strong imagination.   In order to be free from a dis-
temper which renders you miserable, you must not act
like one in despair.   You must be carefull of your
health by living regularly, and carefull of your mind
by employing it moderately.   If you act thus you may
expect to be happy; if you resign yourself to fancy, you
will have, now and then, a little feverish joy, but no
permanent satisfaction.   I should think you should

beleive me. I am no clergyman. I am no physician.
I am not even a lover. I am just a gentleman upon his
travels who has taken an attachment to you and who
has your happiness at heart. I may add, a gentleman
whom you honour with your esteem. My dear Zélide!
You are very good, you are very candid. Pray, forgive me for begging you to be less vain; you have fine
talents of one kind, but are you not deficient in others?
Do you think your *reason* is as distinguished as your
imagination? Beleive me, Zélide, it is not. Beleive
me, and endeavour to improve.

After all this serious counsel, I think my conscience
cannot reproach me for writing to you. I am sure that
your worthy father could not be offended at it. I am
sure that I intend to do you service if I can. . . .

As you and I, Zélide, are perfectly easy with each
other, I must tell you that I am vain enough to read
your letters in such a manner as to imagine that you
realy was in love with me, as much as you can be with
any man. I say *was*, because I am much mistaken if
it is not over before now. Reynst [1] had not judged so
ill. You have no command of yourself. You can conceal nothing. You seemed uneasy. You had a forced
merriment. The Sunday evening that I left you I
could perceive you touched. But I took no notice of
it. From your conversation I saw very well that I had
a place in your heart, that you regarded me with a
warmth more than freindly. Your letters showed me
that you was pleasing yourself with having at last met
with the man for whom you could have a strong and a
lasting passion. But I am too generous not to unde-

---

[1] Zélide's brother.

ceive you.   You are sensible that I am a man of strict
probity.   You have told me so.   I thank you.   I hope
you shall always find me so.   Is it not, however, a little
hard that I have not a better opinion of you?   Own,
Zélide, that your ungoverned vivacity *may* be of dis-
service to you.   It renders you less esteemed by the
man whose esteem you value.   You tell me, "*Je ne
vaudrois rien pour votre femme, je n'ai pas les talens sub-
alternes.*"   If by these talents you mean the domestic
virtues, you will find them necessary for the wife of
every sensible man.   But there are many stronger
reasons against your being my wife, so strong that as I
said to you formerly, I would not be married to you to
be a King.   I know myself and I know you.   And from
all probability of reasoning, I am very certain that if
we were married together, it would not be long before
we should be both very miserable.   My wife must be
a character directly opposite to my dear Zélide, except
in affection, in honesty, and in good humour.   You
may depend upon me as a freind.   It vexes me to think
what a number of freinds you have.   I know, Zélide,
of several people that you correspond with.   I am
therefore not so vain of your corresponding with me.
But I love you, and would wish to contribute to your
happiness.

We may well pause here for breath.   There has
been little enough so far of what is conventionally
regarded as the style of a love-letter; nevertheless,
when a gentleman displays obvious annoyance
because a lady has so many other correspondents,
he may, if a thousand novelists speak the truth,

be regarded as having reached that stage of jealousy to which she has labored to reduce him. It is clear that, whether or not Zélide cared to marry our friend, she was not unwilling that he should languish at her feet. Did she not confess herself a coquette? That she knew how to pique his interest is evident from her very words, which have struck him, as she intended they should do, and which rankle. The talents of a subaltern wife she does not possess. Nor, I venture to think, was it well for Boswell to marry a woman who had them. But let us return to our letter.

You bid me write whatever I think. I ask your pardon for not complying with that request. I shall write nothing that I do not think. But you are not the person to whom I could without reserve write all that I think. After this I shall write in French. Your correspondence will improve me much in that language. You write it charmingly. Am I not very obedient to your orders of writing *des grandes lettres?* You must do the same. While I remain at Berlin, my address is chez Messieurs Splizerber et Daum, Berlin. Adieu. Think and be happy. Pray write soon and continue to show me all your *heart.* I fear all your *fancy.* I fear that the heart of Zélide is not to be found. It has been consumed by the fire of an excessive imagination. Forgive me for talking to you with such an air of authority. I have assumed the person of Mentor. I must keep it up. Perhaps I judge too hardly of you. I think you have cordiality and yet you are much at-

tached to your father and to your brothers. Defend
yourself. Tell me that I am the severe Cato. Tell me
that you will make a very good wife. Let me ask you,
then, Zélide, could you submit your inclinations to the
opinion, perhaps the *caprice*, of a husband? Could
you do this with chearfulness, without losing any of
your sweet good humour, without boasting of it?
Could you live quietly in the country six months a year?
Could you make yourself agreeable to plain honest
neighbours? Could you talk like any other woman,
and have your fancy as much at command as your harpsi-
chord? Could you pass the other six months in a city where
there is very good society, though not the high mode?

At this point the reader interrupts the writer
with cries of protest, *fortissimo*. We all reply
unanimously in the negative. Poor Zélide, you
certainly could *not* do these things, and well did
James Boswell know it. He knew that Zélide
could not be happy at Auchinleck, because he
could not be happy there himself; and if the reader
will have the patience to look once more at the
questions that are asked, he will hear the echoes
of a conversation between James and Zélide, in
which she had been given an account of the manifold miseries of life in Scotland. Withal, the whole
passage is touched with that preposterous humour
to which Boswell liked to feel that his friends
finally became accustomed. But his catechism is
not yet finished.

Could you live thus, and be content? Could you have a great deal of amusement in your own family? Could you give spirits to your husband when he is melancholy? I have known such wives, Zélide. What think you? Could you be such a one? If you can, you may be happy with the sort of man that I once described to you. Adieu.

Let not religion make you unhappy. Think of God as he realy is, and all will appear chearfull. I hope you shall be a Christian. But, my dear Zélide! worship the sun rather than be a Calvinist. You know what I mean. I had sealed this letter. I must break it up and write a little more. This is somewhat like you. I charge you once for all, Be strictly honest with me. If you love me, own it. I can give you the best advice. If you change, tell me. If you love another, tell me. I don't understand a word of your mystery about "a certain gentleman whom you think of three times a day." What do you mean by it? Berlin is a most delightfull city. I am quite happy. I love you more than ever. I would do more than ever to serve you. I would kneel and kiss your hand, if I saw you married to the man that could make you happy. Answer me this one question. If I had pretended a passion for you, which I might easily have done, for it is not difficult to make us beleive what we are allready pleased to imagine — answer me — would you not have gone to the world's end? Supposing even that I had been disinherited by my father, would you not have said, "Sir, here is my portion. It is yours. We may live genteely upon it." Zélide, Zélide, excuse my vanity. But I tell you, you do not know yourself, if you say that you would not have done thus. You see how freely I write, and how proudly. Write you with all freedom, but with your enchanting humility ! *"Je suis glorieuse d'être votre amie."* That is the stile. Is not this a long letter? You must not expect me to write regularly. Farewell, my dear Zélide. Heaven bless you, and make you rationaly happy. Farewell.

This letter, I need scarcely remark, is one of Boswell's most characteristic performances. I have known young ladies to become virtuously indignant over it. There is not in it, we may admit, that note of chivalry which is supposed to indicate a noble devotion to the sex. And yet, when allowance is made for the insolence of it all, for its pomposity and its sermonising, I do not believe that Zélide was displeased with it. Did she not keep it as long as she lived? The very jumble of the sentences in the postscript is eloquent. "I don't understand a word of your mystery of a certain gentleman whom you think of three times a day. What do you mean by it? Berlin is a most delightfull city. I am quite happy. I love you more than ever." If Zélide did not realise that the creature was trapped, she must have been devoid of feminine instinct. If she wanted Boswell, she had but to stoop and pick him up.

For some excellent feminine reason she decided

not to take him at the moment.   She was not sure.
There were other candidates.   And then there
was the thought of living in Scotland, which Boswell had done nothing to make attractive to her.
It was safe to postpone the whole affair.   But she
did not neglect him.   She continued to write to
him, as we know from the fact that Boswell laid
her letters before the philosophic gaze of Rousseau.

During my melancholy at Utrecht [he wrote in
December to Rousseau] I made the acquaintance of a
young woman of the highest nobility, and very rich.   I
conducted myself in such a way as to win the reputation of a philosopher.   Ah, how deceptive are appear-
ances!   If you care to amuse yourself by reading some
pieces by this young lady, you will find them in a small,
separate parcel.   I should like to have your sentiments
on her character.   You are the only one to whom I
have showed her papers.   I could entrust to you anything in the world [*vous confier tout au monde*].

Perhaps Rousseau could not have done better
than to advise Boswell to win Zélide as fast as ever
he could.   Just why James feared her vivacity is
not clear — perhaps it was because she did not
have complete respect for the conventions of
society.   But neither did he.   Marrying a girl
with the same faults that you have yourself has
at least this advantage, that they will not come to

her with a shock of painful novelty, or become an increasing burden with the years. There are people (very modern people) who fancy that Benedick and Beatrice quarrelled and separated soon after their marriage. Certainly they were too wise to live after the conventional standards set by Claudio and Hero. At any rate, I have never heard of any one who thought that they were likely to perish of dulness and boredom. We may quarrel with people constituted like ourselves, but we have also the priceless means of understanding them. Boswell missed the opportunity to marry a girl who understood him. Had they married, she might very probably not have contrived to make of him a steadier or a better man; but I do not think she would have blushed for him. The Boswell family has always been ashamed of the only genius that ever adorned it — a temptation which Zélide, with her more liberal training and temper, might have been depended upon to withstand.

And so Boswell saw Zélide no more. But he could not soon forget her, and she will appear again in our story.

In "sweet Siena," Boswell encountered an "Italian Signora," of a more than earthly beauty, no doubt, who detained him there long after he should have been off to Corsica. Of her we know nothing.

But we do know that the whole problem of our hero's relations with the sex was laid before Paoli; that he gave the finest advice, and also promised Boswell that, if he would return in twenty years, he would find in Corsica, not only science and art, but ladies as splendid as those in any Parisian salon.

CHAPTER VII

WOOING A WIFE

IN the little village of Adamtown, not far from Auchinleck, there lived, in the year 1767, a widow by the name of Blair. Her daughter Kate, the heir to the fortune which had been left by the late Mr. Blair, was eighteen years of age, and described, after the manner of the period, as being sensible, cheerful, and pious, and of a countenance which, though not beautiful, was "agreeable." During her minority her relative, the Laird of Auchinleck, had been one of her guardians; and of a Sunday she sat dutifully in the Master's pew of the little church on the estate.

In the eyes of the young Boswell, just home from his travels, this Scots cousin of his was the finest woman he had ever seen, and her charms were in no way injured by the fact that she possessed great wealth. What a Mistress of Auchinleck she would make! Her picture would adorn the family gallery — "Catherine, wife of James Boswell, Esq., of Auchinleck." Her children would be as clever as their father (or his friend, the Reverend William Temple), and as charming as their mother. Here, at any rate, was a flame of whom one's father might approve. She would, the boy explained, add her lands to the ancestral estates, and he, as her husband, might have, at once, "a pretty little estate, a good house, and a sweet place."

"I wish you had her," said the father laconically.

To her estate James accordingly repaired, and began his suit. He so far succeeded as to prevail upon Mrs. Blair to come and make a visit at Auchinleck, and to bring Kate with her. The visit lasted four days, and there, amid the romantic groves of the family seat, he adored her like a divinity. She was henceforward the "Princess," and before the month of June was out, James rather prematurely referred to her as "my charming bride." When Temple came to Edinburgh to visit the young advocate, he was told that he must ride across country to Adamtown, on a romantic errand, and inspect the goddess. He should have his "consultation guineas" for such expert advice as he, a lifelong friend, knowing the full story of James's foibles, might care to give.

One of the most highly characteristic of Boswellian documents is a sheet of instructions which the young fellow wrote out for his friend, and entitled, "Instructions for Mr. Temple, on his Tour to Auchinleck and Adamtown." It is well known, but we cannot afford to forgo the information that it contains; and a portion of it may be reprinted, as given by its first editor. The sheet has been, unfortunately, separated from the manuscript of which it was originally a part, and its present location is unknown.

He will set out in the fly on Monday morning, and reach Glasgow by noon. Put up at Graham's, and ask for the horses bespoke by Mr. Boswell. Take tickets for the Friday's fly. Eat some cold victuals. Set out for Kingswell, to which you have good road; arrived there, get a guide to put you through the muir to Loudoun; from thence Thomas knows the road to Auchinleck, where the worthy overseer, Mr. James Bruce, will receive you. Be easy with him, and you will like him much; expect but moderate entertainment, as the family is not at home.

Tuesday. — See the house; look at the front; choose your room; advise as to pavilions. Have James Bruce to conduct you to the cab-house; to the old castle; to where I am to make the superb grotto; up the river to Broomsholm; the natural bridge; the grotto; the grotto-walk down to the Gothic bridge; anything else he pleases.

Wednesday. — Breakfast at eight; set out at nine; Thomas will bring you to Adamtown a little after eleven. Send up your name; if possible, put up your horses there; they can have cut grass; if not, Thomas will take them to Mountain, a place a mile off, and come back and wait at dinner. Give Miss Blair my letter. Salute her and her mother; ask to walk. See the place fully; think what improvements should be

made. Talk of my mare, the purse, the chocolate.
Tell you are my very old and intimate friend. Praise
me for my good qualities — you know them; but talk
also how odd, how inconstant, how impetuous, how
much accustomed to women of intrigue. Ask gravely,
"Pray don't you imagine there is something of madness
in that family?" Talk of my various travels — German princes, Voltaire, and Rousseau. Talk of my
father; my strong desire to have my own house. Observe her well. See how amiable! Judge if she would
be happy with your friend. Think of me as the "great
man" at Adamtown — quite classical, too! Study the
mother. Remember well what passes. Stay tea. At
six, order horses, and go to New Mills, two miles from
Loudoun; but if they press you to stay all night, do it.
Be a man of as much ease as possible. Consider what
a romantic expedition you are on. Take notes; perhaps you now fix me for life.

Whether the young clergyman took notes enough
to satisfy the future biographer, and whether he
showed a subtle skill in uniting an indulgent account of Boswell's inconstancy and impetuosity
with a eulogy of his good qualities, I very much
doubt. The rôle of ambassador in affairs of the
heart has ever been fraught with peril; moreover,
Temple was a somewhat stiff and solemn young
man, with a personal — and professional — disap-
proval of Boswell's propensity to intrigue. *He* was
neither odd nor vivacious; and though he loved
his friend for his eccentric charm, it may be

doubted whether he quite succeeded in communicating it.

One incident of Temple's visit was peculiarly alarming. At Adamtown he met a merchant named Fullarton, recently returned from the East Indies, — the whole episode reads like a chapter out of "Roderick Random," — who is thereafter called "the Nabob." His presence there dismayed Boswell, and caused him to cry out, "The mare, the purse, the chocolate, where are they now? . . . I am certainly not deeply in love," he added, "for I am entertained with this dilemma like another chapter in my adventures, though I own to you that I have a more serious attachment to her than I ever had to anybody; for 'here ev'ry flower is united.'"

Boswell had, in truth, got himself into the emotional rapids. The speed at which he was travelling was thrilling, and the constant change of scene and mood afforded him infinite entertainment; but the point towards which he was plunging he could not clearly foresee. To begin with the least of his difficulties, he was still in correspondence with both Zélide and the Italian Signora. The former let him know that she talked of him without either resentment or attachment; the latter wrote "with all the warmth of Italian affection." Kate Blair was better suited to him and to Auchin-

leck, to be sure; but the vivacious Dutch woman
and the passionate Italian offered a life of novelty
and excitement. One of the Signora's letters,
indeed, moved him to tears. And so he fluttered,
in thought, from flower to flower, and tasted the
sweets of each; but he returned ever and anon to
the heiress.

His was an embarrassment of riches. We are
dealing now with the most dissipated period in a
life which was never conspicuous for self-restraint.
It may be questioned whether it is right to bring
to bear against a man the information that is pri-
vately conveyed in a letter to his most intimate
friend, or whether, even after the lapse of a century and a half, a writer is justified in setting down
in cold print the facts that he has read in documents that ought never to have been preserved.
The public is harsh, and the critics are harsher, if
not actually hypocritical, in dealing with erring
mortals who are no longer here to defend themselves or to destroy the evidence against them.
"The important thing," it has been said, "is not
to get caught"; and the adage is as true of the
mighty dead as it is of the living. And yet the
man who has chanced upon new facts in the biography of a great writer may perhaps be pardoned
for giving them to the world; for unless he actually destroys the evidence which he has found

(which of course he has no manner of right to do), he must reckon with the certainty that some later investigator will turn it up and put it into print. The scholar is not responsible for the original recording of the facts; he merely reports what he has found; it is not his office to apportion a great man's meed of praise or infamy. Such a practice has at least the approval of Johnson. When, years later, Boswell proposed to print the autobiography of Sir Robert Sibbald, which he thought "the most natural and candid account of himself that ever was given by any man," Mrs. Thrale objected, and gave the usual reason: "To discover such weakness exposes a man when he is gone." "Nay," said Johnson, "it is an honest picture of human nature."

The fact, then, is that Boswell had sought out the company of other "charmers," notably that of a brunette, whom he habitually describes as his "black friend," and who was known to his friends as "the Moffat woman," because he had met her at the town of that name. Her real name is, fortunately, unknown to us. Temple was eager to get his friend married off, in order to rescue him from this artful female.

I startle [Boswell said to Temple] when you talk of *keeping another man's wife*. Yet that was literally my scheme, though my imagination represented it just as being fond of a pretty, lively, black little lady, who, to oblige me, staid in Edinburgh, and I very genteely paid her expenses. You will see by my letter to her that I shall have a house and a servant-maid upon my hands.

Nevertheless he could not break the disgraceful bond. Perhaps he had neither the will nor the inclination to do so; in any case, he could not do so at the moment, for the woman was about to bear him a child. In December she gave birth to a daughter, who was named "Sally." Boswell makes one reference to her, in a letter to Temple, and then is silent for ever. Of Sally we hear no more.

All this happened in the midst of the negotiations for the hand of the Princess Kate. One can but wonder whether the heiress heard any rumour of the irregularity of her lover's life at the moment when his devotion to her was supposed to be all-absorbing. It is certain that she did hear gossip of another kind. Boswell had been rash in talking about his "Princess" and her "wary mother," and had even spoken of their wish to make a good thing out of any future alliance. This he referred to metaphorically (and indiscreetly) as their system of *salmon-fishing*. Gossip came to the ears of Mrs. Blair, and the Princess, not unnaturally, left Boswell's letters unanswered.

Boswell, too, heard gossip. Miss Blair was, a

friend told him, a well-known jilt. Yet the situation never became so strained as to result in a quarrel. The ladies were, indeed, "wary." Why should they not be so? James was decidedly a good catch, a clever and entertaining young fellow enough, if only, to use his own words, he could restrain his flightiness. It was not necessary, the ladies thought, to break with him; but only to administer a snub. He was allowed to think that the Nabob was winning the day. New rivals appeared. Boswell fretted and fussed. He wrote more letters. At last a temporising reply was sent by the Princess. Her calmness brought him once more to a state of subjection, in which he was convinced that he was at last genuinely in love.

Then, suddenly, Miss Blair burst like a star on Edinburgh, the guest of Lord Kames, the intimate friend and companion of her cousin, Jenny Maxwell, the young Duchess of Gordon. Boswell flew to her at once. She was capricious. At first she seemed glad to see him there. Again, she was distant and reserved. Probably the Duchess had opinions of the suitor which were not without influence. Yet the two were together often. Boswell accompanied the young ladies to the theatre to witness a performance of "Othello," and in the jealous Moor he saw the very likeness of himself. How many a lover has been emboldened by the mimic scene! At this moment he put his arm about her waist, and fancied that she leaned towards him. He watched her tears, and often spoke to her of the torment that they saw before them. Still he thought her distant.

At last the young Duchess went away from Edinburgh, and Boswell was glad of it. He went again to his Princess. The story of his interview is as vivid as anything in the "Life of Johnson."

I found her alone, and she did not seem distant. I told her that I was most sincerely in love with her, and that I only dreaded those faults which I had acknowledged to her. I asked her seriously if she now believed me in earnest. She said she did. I then asked her to be candid and fair as I had been with her, and to tell me if she had any particular liking for me. What think you, Temple, was her answer? "*No;* I really," said she, "have no particular liking for you; I like many people as well as you." (Temple, you must have it in the genuine dialogue.)

BOSWELL. — Do you indeed? Well, I cannot help it. I am obliged to you for telling me so in time. I am sorry for it.

PRINCESS. — I like Jeany Maxwell [Duchess of Gordon] better than you.

B. — Very well. But do you like no man better than me?

P. — No.

B. — Is it possible that you may like me better than other men?

P. — I don't know what is possible.

(By this time I had risen and placed myself by her, and was in real agitation.)

B. — I 'll tell you what, my dear Miss Blair, I love you so much that I am very unhappy. If you cannot love me, I must, if possible, endeavour to forget you. What would you have me do?

P. — I really don't know what you should do.

B. — It is certainly possible that you *may* love me, and if you shall ever do so, I shall be the happiest man in the world. Will you make a fair bargain with me? If you should happen to love me, will you own it?

P. — Yes.

B. — And if you should happen to love another, will you tell me immediately, and help me to make myself easy?

P. — Yes, I will.

B. — Well, you are very good. (Often squeezing and kissing her fine hand, while she looked at me with those beautiful black eyes.)

P. — I may tell you as a cousin what I would not tell to another man.

B. — You may, indeed. You are very fond of Auchinleck — that is one good circumstance.

P. — I confess I am. I wish I liked you as well as I do Auchinleck.

B. — I have told you how fond I am of you. But unless you like me sincerely, I have too much spirit to ask you to live with me, as I know that you do not like me. If I could have you this moment for my wife, I would not.

P. — I should not like to put myself in your offer, though.

B. — Remember, you are both my cousin and my mistress, you must make me suffer as little as possible. As it may happen that I may engage your affections, I should think myself a most dishonourable man, if I were not now in earnest; and, remember, I depend upon your sincerity; and, whatever happens, you and I shall never have any quarrel.

P. — Never.

B. — And I may come and see you as much as I please?

P. — Yes.

O reader, is not this scene worthy of the great Trollope? More modern in tone than Fielding or Fanny Burney? Do you not hear the very language of the eighteenth century more distinctly than in the words of the Narcissas and Sophias who crowd the pages of its fictions? Somehow, I cannot but like the black-eyed Kate. She was a coquette, of course, — much more of a coquette than Zélide, — but I should think all young ladies would be grateful to her for her retort to our hero: "I wish I liked you as well as I do Auchinleck."

Of the art of a man who could thus set down the very words of his courtship in a letter to a friend, not much can be said, for most readers will be thinking rather of the breach of decorum than of the perfection of the art. It would certainly be difficult to discover a passage in any work of fiction which sets forth more vividly the uncertain emotions which surge over a young pair who are discussing the very vital question whether or not they wish to get married. It is all very droll, of course. But then our Boswell was one of the drollest men who ever lived. "Curious" was his own word for the scene: —

My worthy friend, what sort of a scene was this? It was most curious. She said she would submit to her husband in most things. She said that to see one loving her would go far to make her love that person; but she could not talk anyhow positively, for she never had felt the uneasy anxiety of love. We were an hour and a half together, and seemed pleased all the time. I think she behaved with spirit and propriety. I admire her more than ever. . . . She has the justest ideas. She said she knew me now. She could laugh me out of my ill-humour. She could give Lord Auchinleck a lesson how to manage me. Temple, what does the girl mean?

What *did* she mean? It was clear only that she was leading him a chase — he knew not whither. The thought of his rivals dismayed him continually. There was, in particular, a young Member of Parliament, who was also a knight and an officer in the Guards, Sir Alexander Gilmour, said to be worth £1,600 a year. What chance was there with such a competitor? Boswell, who realised

that it would be "a noble match," began to feel
that the game was up.

And then, suddenly, who should appear in Edinburgh but the Nabob! He was himself no happy
suitor, but had concluded, from his own experiences with Kate, that she intended to take Boswell.
This he himself explained to Boswell when they
met. For meet they did. James, it would appear,
scraped acquaintance with Mr. Fullarton by way
of discovering how he stood with the charmer.
The Nabob was all friendliness, and together they
joked about the situation in which they found
themselves. Together they went and called upon
Miss Blair. They were surprised to find that,
though she behaved exceedingly well, her reserve
was more than ordinary. When they left her,
they cried aloud with one accord, "Upon my soul,
a fine woman!"

In a burst of friendly admiration, Boswell proposed that they should sup together at the house
of one of his numerous cousins, and talk matters
over. Perhaps, between them, they could get
something accomplished. "I do believe, Mr. Fullarton," said Boswell, "you and I are in the same
situation here. Is it possible to be upon honour,
and generous, in an affair of this kind?"

They agreed that it was possible. After supper,
they adjourned to a tavern, where we may be

certain that they drank the lady's health, and canvassed the situation. Boswell repeated to Fullarton his friend Dempster's opinion that all Miss Blair's connexions were in an absolute confederacy to lay hold of every man who had a thousand pounds a year, and repeated his own *mot* about the salmon-fishing. "You have hit it," cried the ingenuous Nabob; "we're all kept in play; but I am positive you are the fish, and Sir Alexander is only a mock salmon to force you to jump more expeditiously at the bait." The new allies sat together till two in the morning, by which time they had agreed that both should offer themselves once more to Miss Blair, *privatim et seriatim*. Boswell was to offer first.

In the morning — or, rather, later in the morning — he presented himself once more before the Princess. She received him, and made tea for him. It was well for Boswell that he had come first, for the lady was feeling gracious, though she had apparently decided to put an end to the affair. She begged Mr. Boswell not to be angry, though she must be honest with him. "What, then," said Boswell, "have I no chance?" "No," said she. He asked her to repeat the rejection "upon her word and upon honour," and she did so.

She would not tell me [he adds] whether she was engaged to the knight. She said she would not satisfy an idle curiosity. But I own I had no doubt of it. What amazed me was that she and I were as easy and as good friends as ever. I told her I have great animal spirits, and bear it wonderfully well. But this is really hard. I am thrown upon the wide world again. I don't know what will become of me.

It was, I have said, well for Boswell that he had gone first to try his fortune with the heiress. The other victim got shorter shrift. Alas, poor Nabob! With his appearance on the scene a sudden light must have dawned upon Miss Blair. Despite the "serious and submissive manner" in which the Nabob came to her, she had grown suspicious of collusion; for, as he confided to Boswell, "she would give him no satisfaction, and treated him with a degree of coldness that overpowered him quite."

Well, our Boswell was destined to learn the true nature of a coquette. Zélide had never treated him like this. Perhaps, after all, he had made a mistake. Meanwhile his mind was diverted by a visit to London, where he was delighted to find that he was at last, in truth, "a great man." His "Account of Corsica" had appeared, and had brought him no small amount of fame. He now had his reward for his audacity in visiting the island. A crisis in the fortunes of Paoli and the Corsicans was rapidly approaching; the future of

Corsica was becoming a matter of international significance and public interest. Boswell's book was bought and read. Among other readers was Zélide. She wrote Boswell about the reception of the book in Holland, told him that two Dutch translations were under way, and proposed herself to render the book into French.

Boswell was delighted. Zélide was a woman worth knowing! Correspondence with her flourished once more. "Upon my soul, Temple, I must have her!" he wrote in March. "She is so sensible, so accomplished, and knows me so well, and likes me so much, that I do not see how I can be unhappy with her." He had persuaded his godfather, Sir John Pringle, who had seen Zélide on the Continent, that she was perfectly adapted to him, and wrote to his father begging permission to go over to Utrecht and propose. He had already broached the matter to Zélide, and she had suggested that they meet without having pledged themselves in any way, and see whether they would dare to risk an engagement — if not, they might still be friends for life. "My dear friend," she wrote a little later, "it is prejudice that has kept you so much at a distance from me. If we meet, I am sure that prejudice will be removed."

But Temple, being a clergyman and English,

disapproved of the foreign woman. ("What would
you think of the fine, healthy, amiable Miss Dick,
with whom you dined so agreeably?" Boswell
asked Temple, parenthetically.) And then he sent
Zélide's next letter to his father, that the Laird
might see for himself what a lady she was.

How do we know but she is an inestimable prize?
[he wrote to Temple in April]. Surely it is worth while
to go to Holland to see a fair conclusion, one way or
other, of what has hovered in my mind for years. I
have written to her, and told her all my perplexity. I
have put in the plainest light what conduct I absolutely
require of her; and what my father will require. I have
bid her be my wife at present, and comfort me with a
letter in which she shall shew at once her wisdom, her
spirit, and her regard for me. You shall see it. I tell
you, man, she knows and values me as you do. After
reading the enclosed letters, I am sure you will be better
disposed towards my charming Zélide.

How arrogant is man! Zélide took offence at
last, and sent to Boswell an "acid epistle," the
flashing wit of which, he complained to Temple,
scorched him. She was a lady, brilliant enough,
to be sure, but likely to become a termagant at
forty — and already she was near thirty. Suddenly a fear attacked him that his father would
consent to his proposal to go over to Utrecht and
woo. But luckily Lord Auchinleck was firm. He

would have no Dutch women at Auchinleck; and
so his son now gladly obeyed his behest to let the
woman alone. "Worthy man!" cried the boy,
"this will be a solace to him upon his circuit."

As for Zélide [he wrote to Temple] I have written to
her that we are agreed. "My pride," say I, "and your
vanity would never agree. It would be like the scene
in our burlesque comedy, 'The Rehearsal': 'I am the
bold thunder,' cries one; 'the quick lightning I,' cries
another. *Et voilà notre ménage*." But she and I will
allways be good correspondents.

This final renunciation occurred in May, 1768,
more than four years after the establishment of
their intimacy at Utrecht.

How Boswell weathered it out till summer, it is
not easy to say; he was now, to use his own words,
"thrown upon the world again." But a man who
unites with an extreme susceptibility a fixed determination to marry cannot be long bereaved. In
the course of a visit to his cousins, the Montgom-
erys of Lainshaw, he met the "finest creature that
ever was formed," and named her at once *la belle
Irlandaise*. She was an Irish cousin of Margaret
Montgomery, and so no time need be lost in pre-
liminaries. She had a sweet countenance, full
of sensibility, and was "formed like a Grecian
nymph"; her age was sixteen. Her father (who
had an estate of £1000 a year and "above £10,000

in ready money") was an Irish counsellor-at-law,
and as worthy a man as Boswell had ever met.
Father, mother, and aunt were all in Scotland with
la belle Irlandaise, whose name was Mary Anne.
Father, mother, and aunt all approved of James.
"Mr. Boswell," said the aunt to him, "I tell you
seriously there will be no fear of this succeeding,
but from your own inconstancy." It was arranged that Boswell should visit Ireland in March,
and, furthermore, that in the meantime he should
correspond — with the father.

The thought of a visit to Ireland added a glow
to wooing; the theatre of his adventures was
widening once more. The "Account of Corsica"
was being printed in Ireland, — a so-called "third
edition," — and its success had given the father
and mother — Boswell seems habitually to have
encountered "wary" parents — an opportunity
of flattering the suitor.

From morning to night, I admired the charming Mary
Anne. Upon my honour, I never was so much in love.
I never was before in a situation to which there was
not some objection; *but here ev'ry flower is united,* and
not a thorn to be found. But how shall I manage it?
They were in a hurry, and are gone home to Ireland.
They were sorry they could not come to see Auchinleck,
of which they had heard a great deal. Mary Anne
wished much to be in the grotto. It is a pity they did
not come. This Princely Seat would have had some

effect. . . . I was allowed to walk a great deal with Miss. I repeated my fervent passion to her again and again. She was pleased, and I could swear that her little heart beat. I carved the first letter of her name on a tree. I cut off a lock of her hair, *male pertinaci*. She promised not to forget me, nor to marry a lord before March."

Temple was not the only friend who heard of the passion for Miss Mary Anne. The whole story was confided to Sir Alexander and Lady Dick. The latter had reached the cynical conclusion, shared perhaps by the reader, that Boswell was eager to marry money. Of this sordid motive Boswell speaks in a letter to Sir Alexander, a paragraph of which is here printed for the first time. The reader may make what he can of it.

The Irish heiress whom I went to see at Lainshaw turned out to be the finest creature that ever I beheld, a perfect Arcadian shepherdess, not seventeen; so that instead of solid plans of fortune-hunting, I thought of nothing but the enchanting reveries of gallantry. It was quite a fairy tale. I know that if I were to tell this to Lady Dick, she would not believe a word of it, but would maintain that I am disguising, even to myself, my old passion for gold. The truth, however, is that I am in love as much as ever man was, and if I played Carrickfergus once before, I play it a hundred times now.

I was lately at Adamtown, and had a long talk with

Heiress Kate by the side of her wood.   She told me that
the knight Sir Sawney was never to rule her territories.
But alas, what could I say to her while my heart was
beyond the sea?   So much for love!

A very dangerous relapse, however, in favour of
the Princess now occurred.   Sir Alexander Gilmour
(or Sir Sawney, as Boswell had nicknamed him) had
made off, and the wary mother, it seems, was not
unwilling that James should again be received as a
suitor.   Once more, therefore, did he walk "whole
hours" with Miss Blair, and once again did he
kneel before her.   Letters were written in the old
manner, designed to melt down Kate's coldness.
And then "came a kind letter from my amiable
Aunt Boyd in Ireland, and all the charms of sweet
Marianne revived."

This was in December.   In the spring, somewhat
later than had originally been intended, the proposed visit to Ireland was made.   Boswell had, as
a companion, his cousin Margaret Montgomery,
the particular friend of Mary Anne; at Margaret's
home in Lainshaw, it will be recalled, he had first
met *la belle Irlandaise*.   It is odd that Boswell
should have said so little of this visit.   It is not
mentioned in the "Life of Johnson."   Indeed,
practically nothing has been known hitherto of
Boswell's visit to that remarkable island; but the
discovery of a letter to Sir Alexander Dick, written

from Donaghadee, on May 29, 1769, lights up the whole of this obscure period in Boswell's life. In Ireland Boswell ran true to form. He was careful to meet the Lord Lieutenant. Why should one cross the Irish Sea and fail to meet the most prominent man in the nation? But how to approach a lord lieutenant? As a friend of Corsica. Nothing more natural. By this device he had obtained an interview with William Pitt, the Prime Minister of England, three years before, when he had called on the great man, dressed in Corsican costume, and pleaded for his foreign friends. He now found the Irish naturally well disposed towards the Corsicans.

The Lord Lieutenant was remarkably good to me [he writes]. And I assure you I have not met a firmer and keener Corsican. I believe something considerable will be raised in this kingdom for the brave islanders. I am indefatigable in fanning the generous fire. I have lately received a noble, spirited letter from Paoli. This I have shewn to numbers, and it has had an admirable effect.

Boswell liked the country as well as the people. He thought Dublin "a noble city," and the life there "magnificent." He visited a number of country seats, and saw some rich and well-cultivated land. He planned, before his return, to visit Lough Neach and the Giants' Causeway.

Boswell in Corsican Attire

In the dress of an armed Corsican Chief, as he appeared at Shakespeare's Jubilee
at Stratford-on-Avon, September, 1769, the year following his publication of
" An Account of Corsica "

He would like, he said, to come back and see a "great deal more of Hibernia."

But what of Mary Anne? A study of this young lady in her native land does not seem in any way to have diminished her charms. During this period no letters were written to Temple, so that we miss the opportunity to follow every shift in the lover's mood. But the confidences reposed in Sir Alexander Dick are no less frank, though much less voluminous.

I must not forget *la belle Irlandaise*, who is really as amiable as I told you I thought her. Only figure me dancing a jig (or strathspey) with her to the tune of Carrickfergus, played by an Irish piper.

This, I regret to say, is the last of Boswell's utterances about the Irish beauty. What it was that cooled the ardour of the young people we do not know; we must await the discovery of other letters written in the early summer of 1769. Perhaps the parents put an end to the affair. Be this as it may, before the month of June was out, Boswell was engaged to be married to his cousin, Margaret Montgomery, who had accompanied him on the Irish expedition.

Could anything be more unexpected? Hitherto, in Boswell's correspondence, Margaret had been a mere lay figure; not once is she mentioned in connexion with love. She was a quiet and admira-

ble person, of whom Boswell's elders must have
approved. They must have deemed her an eminently safe person — was she not a cousin? She
was not a foreign woman, who would introduce a
strange note into the society of Auchinleck; she
was not wealthy, but she would do. It was really
essential to get James married off. Since his
return from the Continent, his life had been growing ever looser. There was need of a steady, feminine hand. Therefore, it would seem, they took
care to throw him with Margaret, trusting in the
effect of propinquity. Even before the expedition
to Ireland, Boswell speaks to Sir Alexander of Miss
Montgomery as sitting by him while he writes.
Sir Alexander himself lent his influence to the
plans that the family were working out. He told
Boswell that he would find his cousin's conversation "nutritive," and the word pleased the young
man. "Indeed it is such as nourished me," he
replied, "and like sweet milk tempers and smooths
my agitated mind."

Mrs. Boswell was one of those kindly, long-
suffering women whose lives are a quiet blessing
to men; unhonoured by the world, but eternally
dear to a few who are privileged to be near them.
Through a long wedded life, through years in
which bitterness must have been her portion, she
was a devoted wife to Boswell. He loved her, and

after her death never ceased, in his own garrulous fashion, to lament her loss.

But her husband's ways were not her ways. His enthusiasms she could not share. It is to be feared that his restless hero-hunting was to her a source of shame. At the very best, it could have seemed no better to her than the eccentric taste of a man who collects exotic animals as pets. "She disapproved," says Boswell, "of my inviting Mr. M——sh, a man of ability but of violent manners, to make one in a genteel party at our house one evening. 'He is,' said she, 'like fire and water, useful but not to be brought into company.'" Mrs. Boswell was not interested in making social experiments, in mixing different kinds. She would never have seated Samuel Johnson and John Wilkes at the same table. In a word, she never really understood what her husband was about, and never assisted him in developing that very strange variety of genius which Nature had bestowed upon him.

Just at the end of Boswell's Commonplace Book there is a sheet headed, "Uxoriana." It is one of the most pathetic pages ever traced by his cheerful pen, for it is his attempt to Boswellise his wife. Its pathos, to my mind, consists in its brevity — there are but four anecdotes set down, and they are dull. There was in the lady nothing to

Boswellise.   Did he ever, I wonder, in the long dull evenings at Edinburgh and at Auchinleck, let his mind wander back to the Utrecht days, and to a young woman who had told him that she did not have the talent to become a subaltern in his life ?

CHAPTER VIII

THE SOCIAL GENIUS OF BOSWELL

I suppose that the simplest manifestation of social genius is a desire of getting people together and exposing them to one another. Our interest in drama and novel consists largely in seeing people whom we know brought into contact with strange or hostile persons, so that they may exhibit or develop new sides of themselves. It is hard to interest a reader in the unbroken serenities of family life. It is hard for social genius to content itself with the domestic circle. A man endowed with such a genius is perpetually hankering after "new faces, other minds"; he finds in clubs and crowded drawing-rooms a varied and coloured life which puts to shame the modest pleasures of solitude and meditation.

All intellectual improvement arises, perhaps, from submitting ourselves to men and to ways of life that are originally alien to us; if, in time, they get the better of our conservatism, our life is clearly the better for the enrichment they have given it; but if, on the other hand, we are in the end obliged to repudiate them, we retire with the renewed strength that arises from opposition, and our second state is better than our first. If you happen, for example, to dislike Frenchmen, it would, according to this philosophy, be well for you to go and live among Frenchmen until you discover whether you are right. If you find yourself becoming a snob or a Pharisee, it might be well for you to go among criminals and mendicants, until you realise the fascination of the irregular life. An hour's experience in such matters is worth more than a year of meditations.

Of this philosophy of exposure James Boswell was ever an ardent disciple. He loved friction — the excitement which arises from the sudden contact of rivals, the collision of opponents, ill-assorted companies : Jove among peasants, Samuel Johnson in the Hebrides. He let his imagination play with the thought of bringing Rousseau and Voltaire together. In his youth he went into the company of actors and of Roman Catholics, because actors and Roman Catholics were not approved of by the stern society in which he had been reared ; in his maturer years he courted the acquaintance of the notorious Mrs. Margaret Caroline Rudd, who had barely escaped from the fangs of the law when the Perreau brothers were hanged for forgery ; and he rode to the place of execution with the Reverend Mr. Hackman, the murderer.

Over these incidents the biographers and critics of Boswell have made merry, or wagged their heads with indignation. There is, however, something to be said for knowing human nature, even in its most unpopular, or even criminal, manifestations; one may hazard the opinion that the critics themselves would be the wiser for some knowledge of the unconventional life. What if Boswell did write an amatory song to Mrs. Rudd? It was because he felt her charm; and I do not doubt that she had more of it than all the bluestockings and dowagers in Scotland. Johnson himself envied Boswell his acquaintance with Mrs. Rudd.

There were, Boswell discovered, easy ways of introducing into conversation this necessary friction. One can always take the other side, whether he belongs on it or not. One can always affect ignorance or prejudice. This was, from the beginning, one of his favourite methods of drawing a man out. "I ventured," he writes of Paoli, "to reason like a libertine, that I might be confirmed in virtuous principles by so illustrious a preceptour. I made light of moral feelings. I argued that conscience was vague and uncertain; that there was hardly any vice but what men might be found who have been guilty of it without remorse." This from the man who wrote reams of the most excellent counsel to Zélide! Yet, in the midst of his *g*[d]

James Boswell.
Oxford 1776.

This pious Treatise
used to be ~~read~~ *by*
my excellent Mother.
I was glad to buy a
copy of it, at Oxford.

Boswell's Inscription in a copy of Anthony Horneck's "The Fire of the Altar, or Certain Directions how to raise the Soul into Certain Flames, before, at, and after the Receiving the Blessed Sacrament" sermon to Zélide, he had cried out, "Defend yourself. Tell me that I am the severe Cato."

The record of Johnson's conversation teems with illustrations of Boswell's skill in starting or directing the flow of talk. When Johnson expatiated on the advantages to Scotland of the union with England, Boswell himself was delighted with the "copious exaggeration" of the talk, but he feared the effect of it on the Scotch listeners. "I therefore," says he, "diverted the subject." He talked with Mr. Gerard on the "difference of genius," for the express purpose of engaging him and Johnson in a discussion of the subject. On another occasion he wrote: "A strange thought struck me, to try if he knew anything of . . . the trade of a butcher. I enticed him into the subject."

Again, he was eternally asking questions. How else, pray, is one to discover the extent of another's conversation? Recall that fascinating vision which he summoned up, of Johnson shut into a tower with a new-born baby. "Sir, what would you do? Would you take the trouble of rearing it? Would you teach it anything?" And (doubtless as growing out of this very subject), "Is natural affection born with us? Is marriage natural to man?" Here is an interlocutor by no means profound, but eager and curious, full of novel expedients for waking his subject into activity, spurring, enticing, decoying him, and playing the fool before him.

I also [he wrote] may be allowed to claim some merit in leading the conversation. I do not mean leading, as in an orchestra, by playing the first fiddle; but leading as one does in examining a witness — starting topics, and making him pursue them.

It is a felicitous comparison. Boswell had the ingenuity of a lawyer trained in cross-examination and in wringing a subject dry. There is much also in the musical metaphor which he abandons. He *is* very like a performer on a musical instrument. By skilful manipulation, he plays upon men so as to display all that is most characteristic in them. Of this peculiar skill he was fully aware, and loved to analyse it. He had learned, for example, how to play upon John Wilkes, and he so far divulged the secret as to write thus to the man himself :—

Philosophy can analyse human nature, and from every man of parts can extract a certain quantity of good. Dare I affirm that I have found chearfulness, knowledge, wit, and generosity even in Mr. Wilkes? I suppose few crucibles are so happily constructed as mine, and I imagine that I have a particular talent for finding the gold in your Honour's composition. Certain it is that the process must be performed very delicately.

Another passage on the same theme makes use of a metaphor much less felicitous, but is certainly of value in showing the conscious art of which Boswell was the master.   It is drawn from the Commonplace Book, and reads: —

My friends are to me like the cinnamon tree, which produces nutmeg, mace, and cinnamon; not only do I get wisdom and worth out of them, but amusement.   I use them as the Chinese do their animals; nothing is lost; there is a very good dish made of the poorest parts. So I make the follies of my friends serve as a dessert after their valuable qualities.

Of the splendour of this endowment it is perhaps hardly necessary to speak.   To influence men in such a way as to bring into life whatever is most characteristic; to appreciate and elicit whatever is best in the man before you; to make his true qualities triumph over his inertia and his conventionality, is, in the fullest sense, surely a creative act. Boswell could almost boast that he taught men to know themselves.

Because of this more serious purpose, he cared but little for mere pyrotechnical display in conversation.   There were, in his immediate circle, three men famous for epigrams and *bons mots*,—Beauclerk, Garrick, and Richard Brinsley Sheridan, — yet he never cared to make a collection of their witty remarks. Wit, of course, he delighted in;

but the highest form of wit is that in which it blends with wisdom, and in which it leads the inquirer on to a subtler consideration of the subject, or provides a sharp summary of it in some flash of inspiration. In Corsica, Paoli had said to him, "Je ne puis souffrir longtemps les diseurs de bons mots"; whereupon Boswell comments: —

How much superiour is this great man's idea of agreeable conversation to that of professed wits, who are continually straining for smart remarks and lively repartees. They put themselves to much pain in order to please, and yet please less than if they would just appear as they naturally feel themselves. A company of professed wits has always appeared to me like a company of artificers employed in some very nice and difficult work, which they are under a necessity of performing.

It is because of this neglect of mere repartee that the conversation recorded by Boswell never impresses the reader as a jest-book or a collection of unset jewels. There is plenty of relief. It is his glory to have given us the gem in its setting.

For a somewhat similar reason there is in his letters a lack of mere news. He is not a great letter-writer, for letter-writing to him is seldom an end in itself. He usually has some secondary purpose in mind. He may wish to ask a favour, or, as in conversation, to draw out the real man.

The following letter to Goldsmith, never before printed, is an excellent example of the art I have been attempting to define. It was written immediately after news of the first performance of "She Stoops to Conquer" had reached Boswell in Scotland. The success of the piece had vastly enhanced Goldsmith's reputation, and Boswell was filled with longing to witness and record the triumph, to get into correspondence with the new dramatist, to persuade him to write him a letter spontaneously — and that quickly, "as if in repartee." There is no telling what may come of such a correspondence. Perhaps he had not been quite fair to Goldsmith, who may respond, in the hour of success, to the Boswellian stimulus. Who knows but what he may yet wish to Boswellise him?

But no. Goldsmith was no letter-writer. Specimens of his letters are of unexampled rarity. His published correspondence does not extend to forty letters. He had no time for letter writing — least of all with Boswell. He had time only for Newbery. But this makes all the more interesting the following example, which, so far as known, is the only letter that ever passed between them.

It begins with a characterisation of that depressing type of sentimental comedy on which "She Stoops to Conquer" had been an attack. It would be difficult, I think, in the range of criticism to find

Dear Sir

Edinburgh
29 March 1773.

I sincerely wish you joy on the great success of your new Comedy: She Stoops to conquer, or the mistakes of a night. The English Nation was just falling into a lethargy. Their blood was thickened and their minds creamed and mantled like a standing Pool; and no wonder, when their Comedies which should enliven them, like sparkling Champagne, were become mere syrup of poppies gentle soporifick draughts. Had there been no interruption to this, our audiences must have gone to the Theatres with their night caps. In the Opera houses abroad, the Boxes are fitted up for tea drinking Those at Drury Lane & Covent Garden must have been furnished with settees, and

commodiously

Facsimile of Letter of Congratulation

Written by Boswell to Goldsmith on the happy coincidence of the first production of " She Stoops to Conquer " and the birth of his own daughter

commodiously adjusted for repose. I
am happy to hear that you have waked
the spirit of mirth which has so long layn
dormant, and revived natural humour
and hearty laughter It gives me pleasure
that our friend Garrick has written the
Prologue for you. It is at least lending
you a Postilion since you have not
his coach; and I think it is a very
good one, admirably adapted both to
the Subject and to the Authour of the
Comedy.

    You must know my wife was safely
delivered of a daughter, the very evening
that She stoops to conquer first appeared
I am fond of the coincidence. My little
daughter is a fine healthy lively child,
and I flatter myself shall be blest
with the cheerfullness of your Comick Muse.
                                        She

She has nothing of that wretched whining and crying which we see children so often have; nothing of the Comedie Larmoyante. I hope she shall live to be an agreable companion, and to diffuse gayety over the days of her father, which are sometimes a little cloudy.

I intend being in London this spring and promise myself great satisfaction in sharing your social hours. In the mean time, I beg the favour of hearing from you. I am sure you have not a warmer friend or a steadier admirer While you are in the full glow of Theatrical Splendour, while all the great and the gay in the British Metropolis are literally hanging upon your smiles, let me see that you can stoop to write to me.

I ever am with great regard Dear Sir your affectionate humble servant

James Boswell.

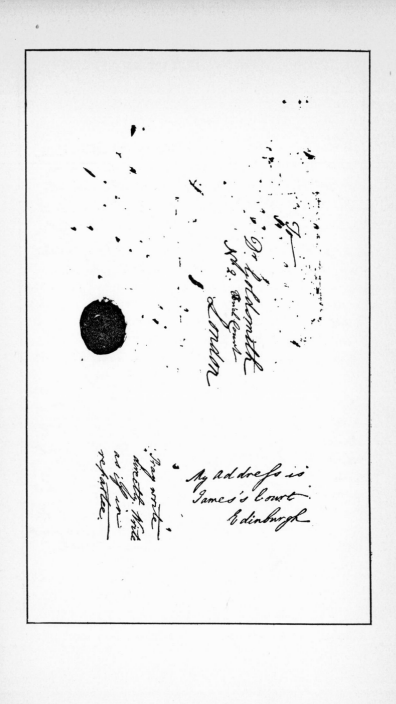

To
Dr. Goldsmith
No. 2, Brick Court
London

My address is
James's Court
Edinburgh

Pray write
directly, that
we if we
separate.

a more sprightly account of the *comédie larmoyante* of the eighteenth century.

EDINBURGH, 29 *March* 1773.

DEAR SIR, —

I sincerely wish you joy on the great success of your new comedy, *She stoops to conquer, or the mistakes of a night*. The English Nation was just falling into a lethargy. Their blood was thickened and their minds *creamed and mantled like a standing pool;* and no wonder — when their Comedies which should enliven them, like sparkling Champagne, were become mere syrup of poppies gentle, soporifick draughts. Had there been no interruption to this, our audiences must have gone to the Theatres with their night caps. In the opera houses abroad, the Boxes are fitted up for teadrinking. Those at Drury Lane & Covent Garden must have been furnished with settees, and commodiously adjusted for repose. I am happy to hear that you have waked the spirit of mirth which has so long layn dormant, and revived natural humour and hearty laughter. It gives me pleasure that our friend Garrick has written the Prologue for you. It is at least lending you a Postilion, since you have not his coach; and I think it is a very good one, admirably adapted both to the Subject and to the Authour of the Comedy.

There is reference here to the fact that "She Stoops to Conquer" was performed, not at Garrick's theatre, the Drury Lane, but at the Covent Garden. Of this fact Walpole wrote sneeringly:

" Garrick would not act it, but bought himself off with a poor prologue." Boswell, however, liked what Walpole detested, and was glad Goldsmith might have a prologue by Garrick if he could not have the advantage of a production at the Drury Lane under the personal supervision of his famous friend.

The next paragraph furnishes a specimen of Boswell's humour than which none is better.

You must know my wife was safely delivered of a daughter, the very evening that *She stoops to conquer* first appeared. I am fond of the coincidence. My little daughter is a fine healthy lively child, and I flatter myself shall be blest with the cheerfullness of your Comick Muse. She has nothing of that wretched whining and crying which we see children so often have; nothing of the *Comedie Larmoyante.* I hope she shall live to be an agreable companion, and to diffuse gayety over the days of her father, which are sometimes a little cloudy.

I intend being in London this spring, and promise myself great satisfaction in sharing your social hours. In the mean time, I beg the favour of hearing from you. I am sure you have not a warmer friend or a steadier admirer. While you are in the full glow of Theatrical Splendour, while all the great and the gay in the British metropolis are literally hanging upon *your smiles,* let me see that you can *stoop to write* to me.

I ever am, with great regard, Dear Sir,
        Your affectionate, humble servant,
                    JAMES BOSWELL.
My address is James's Court, Edinburgh.
Pray write directly.   Write as if in repartee.

The high opinion which I have expressed of Boswell's influence will seem to many extreme; but in any critical essay on Boswell, it is necessary to account for a unique thing — his genius. An exceptionally high estimate is indispensable if one is to account for genius. And yet there would be something quite inadequate in the analysis if we stopped here. We must beware of neglecting what Boswell called his "romantic imagination." Boswell's wayward imagination might almost be taken as an illustration of Keats's injunction ever to let the fancy roam. He was particularly fond of imagining himself in romantic circumstances.

Readers of the "Life of Johnson" will not have forgotten the evening on which Johnson and Boswell listened to a fiddler at Ashbourne. "I told him," writes Boswell, "that it [the power of music] affected me to such a degree as often to agitate my nerves painfully, producing in my mind alternate sensations of pathetick dejection, so that I was ready to shed tears, and of daring resolution, so that I was inclined to rush into the thickest part of the battle."

Boswell was plainly right in calling this "romantic." If Rousseau had written the sentence, or Berlioz, it would have been cited as a typical illustration of glorious self-abandonment to exalted, perhaps unearthly, emotions. Johnson's reply,

"Sir, I should never hear it if it made me such a fool," shows that he was no wiser than the rest of the world in interpreting this fantastic quality of Boswell's.   Boswell had, at times, longings worthy of a Byron.   He confided — rashly — to Johnson that he was sometimes in the humour of wishing to retire to a "desart"; and he wrote to Temple that he could be "whinstone on the face of a mountain," were it possible for him to be conscious of it and to "brave the elements by glorious insensibility." There is a typical bit of romanticism, full half a century before Byron cried aloud to the Alpine night, —

> Let me be
> A sharer in thy fierce and far delight,
> A portion of the tempest and of thee.

After dining with Captain Cook, Boswell felt a desire to join him on his next expedition, and perhaps circumnavigate the globe.   At another time he longed to go and see the Great Wall of China. However truly Boswell may be the exponent of the Age of Prose and its crowded life in salon and club, he was no less a child of the Romantic Movement.   And he who does not realise that Boswell's love of the civilisation of his own time is for ever crossed and altered by strange yearnings after something larger, simpler, and more emotional has utterly failed to understand him.   To say that this was inconsistent is but to assert once more that it was romantic.

As for himself, he realised it as fully as might be. Indeed, he never tired of talking about it; but the people among whom he lived did not suffer from incomprehensible romantic longings for a larger experience. His own description of this side of his mind will be found in the Commonplace Book.

Boswell, who had a good deal of whim, used not only to form wild projects in his imagination, but would sometimes reduce them to practice. In his calm hours, he said, with great good humour, "There have been many people who built castles in the air, but I believe I am the first that ever attempted to live in them."

It will be remembered that he told Rousseau that he often formed "des plans romanesques, jamais des plans impossibles."

One of Boswell's plans that was almost realised was a "scheme of going up the Baltick." Johnson was inclined to it, and Boswell never forgave himself for not carrying it out. His words of regret are characteristic of him in more ways than one : —

I am sorry now that I did not insist on our executing that scheme. Besides the other objects of curiosity and observation, to have seen my illustrious friend received, as he probably would have been, by a Prince so eminently distinguished for his variety of talents and acquisitions as the late King of Sweden; and by the

Empress of Russia, whose extraordinary abilities, information, and magnanimity astonish the world, would have afforded a noble subject for contemplation and record. The reflection may possibly be thought too visionary by the more sedate and cold-blooded part of my readers; yet I own, I frequently indulge it with an earnest, unavailing regret.

But it is not necessary to accept Boswell's statement that he alone attempted to go and live in his Spanish castles. Have not the greatest dreamers always done so? Is not every great achievement a bit romantic in its first conception? Certainly it is true that every one of Boswell's achievements was, in the beginning, a somewhat crack-brained dream. It was foolish and visionary for him, at the age of twenty-one, to dream of becoming the intimate companion of the King of Letters in London — and the dream came true. It was a crazy notion to go to Corsica when it was in a state of insurrection, in order to scrape acquaintance with the rebel leader and interpret his plans to the world; therefore he went and did it. It was rash, almost to the verge of madness, to take Dr. Samuel Johnson, aged sixty-four, on a jaunt to Ultima Thule; but he did it — to the delight of the world. And so it is important for those who call Boswell a fool to sit down and meditate on the whole nature of folly. Unless they are prepared to deny his genius altogether, they must realise that it was inseparably bound up with this romantic folly of his, which, when its airy castles prove to be of solid substance, has a very different look.

To realise one of his dreams was to Boswell the keenest delight in the world. At such a moment his spirit knew no bounds. When, for example, he had got Johnson into a hackney-coach *en route* for the Wilkes dinner, he "exulted as much as a fortune-hunter who has got an heiress into a post-chaise with him to set out for Gretna-Green." When he realised that he had actually got Johnson to the Hebrides, his elation was so great that he compared himself to "a dog who has got hold of a large piece of meat, and runs away with it to a corner, where he may devour it in peace." An illustration of what he himself called his "avidity for delight" may be given from a letter addressed to Samuel Johnson from the town of Chester. He was on his way down to Scotland, and had stopped to visit his friend, Colonel Stuart. Here the fascination of the martial life mingled with the dignity of the ecclesiastical life (for he was graciously received by Bishop Porteus) to produce a very draught of "mortal felicity."

Your letter, so full of polite kindness and masterly counsel, came like a large treasure upon me, while already glittering with riches. I was quite enchanted

at Chester, so that I could with difficulty quit it.   But
the enchantment was the reverse of that of Circe, for
so far was there from being any thing sensual in it, that
I was *all mind*.   I do not mean all reason only; for my
fancy was kept finely in play.   And why not? — If you
please I will send you a copy, or an abridgement of my
Chester journal, which is truly a log-book of felicity.

There is in this quotation every characteristic
mark of Boswell's genius.   He has, to begin with,
met everybody in Chester.   He has received a
letter from Samuel Johnson, which he has of course
shown to the Bishop, and has become at once "the
Great Man."   He has filled his mind by conversation with the great, and yet he has fed his fancy
as well as his reason.   And finally, he has got a
record of it all.   No wonder he was in such spirits
that he hoped to be able to vanquish even the
black dog of melancholy that would meet him at
home.

It was this well-spring of gaiety that recom-
mended Boswell to his friends.   He reckoned with
it as one of his chief qualities.   There was not
much, in the eyes of the great, to recommend the
young man, and he knew it.   Therefore he made
the more skilful use of such endowments as he
possessed.   It will be remembered that, when he
was first admitted to the presence of Paoli, the
General could not understand why the young man

was there; he suspected the presence of a spy, and was on his guard. But Boswell disarmed him at last. He talked flatteringly about a possible alliance between Britain and Corsica. "I insensibly got the better of his reserve upon this head. My flow of gay ideas relaxed his severity and brightened up his humour."

It was to this perpetual good humour that Boswell owed all his social success. The social honour that he coveted most, election to the great Literary Club, he owed to this. In the remoteness of the Highlands Johnson confessed to Boswell that several had wished to keep him out of the Club. "Burke told me, he doubted if you were fit for it; but, now you are in, none of them are sorry. Burke says that you have so much good humour naturally, it is scarce a virtue."

Nobody is likely to accuse Samuel Johnson of being a flatterer, yet he told Boswell that he was a man whom everybody liked. The harsh criticism of him, as insolent and pushing, comes from people who were never sufficiently in contact with him to be won by his infectious gaiety. It may, indeed, be doubted whether there are any social restrictions that will not go down before indomitable good humour. Under its warm influence pride of place is forgotten, and mortals permit themselves to take pleasure in one another rather than in the barriers which they have reared about their self-importance.

Two excellent examples of this power of Boswell's are set down by Fanny Burney in her "Diary." Few persons were more adequately equipped with a sense of etiquette than the fluttering little lady whose diary is greater than any of her novels. The first anecdote was written at the time when she was enslaved at Windsor, wearing her life out in curtsying to Queen Charlotte and answering the idiotic questions of King George. Boswell, like the rest of Miss Burney's friends, had grown indignant at this, and determined, even at the cost of scandal, to release her from her confinement. Boswell, who had known her well at Streatham in the days before Johnson's death, approached her through the Reverend Mr. Giffardier, whose acquaintance we made in the second chapter of this book, and whom Miss Burney always called by the sobriquet of Mr. Turbulent.

[Mr. Turbulent] proposed bringing him to call upon me; but this I declined, certain how little satisfaction would be given here by the entrance of a man so famous for compiling anecdotes. But yet I really wished to see him again for old acquaintance' sake, and unavoidable amusement from his oddity and good humour, as well as respect for the object of his constant admiration, my revered Dr. Johnson. I therefore told Mr. Turbulent

I should be extremely glad to speak with him after the service was over.

Accordingly, at the gate of the choir, Mr. Turbulent brought him to me. We saluted with mutual glee; his comic-serious face and manner have lost nothing of their wonted singularity, nor yet have his mind and language, as you will soon confess.

"I am extremely glad to see you, indeed," he cried, "but very sorry to see you here. My dear ma'am, why do you stay? — it won't do, ma'am! you must resign! — we can put up with it no longer. I told my good host, the Bishop, so last night; we are all grown quite outrageous!"

Whether I laughed the most or stared the most, I am at a loss to say.

The conversation is much longer than this; but as it is familiar to many readers, it need not be reproduced in its entirety. Boswell attempted to enlist Miss Burney's assistance in the collection of material for the "Life of Johnson," but she did not feel that she could give it. The publication of the book, in 1791, shocked and grieved her by its frankness. She was angry at the author, and remained so until she finally met him at Mrs. Ord's, where he was the guest of honour at dinner.

This last [Mr. Boswell] was the object of the morning. I felt a strong sensation of that displeasure which his loquacious communications of every weakness and infirmity of the first and greatest good man of these times have awakened in me at his first sight; and though his address to me was courteous in the extreme, and he made a point of sitting next me, I felt an indignant disposition to a nearly forbidding reserve and silence. . . . Angry, however, as I have long been with him, he soon insensibly conquered, though he did not soften me. There is so little of ill-design or ill-nature in him, he is so open and forgiving for all that is said in return, that he soon forced me to consider him in a less serious light, and change my resentment against his treachery into something like commiseration of his levity; and before we parted, we became good friends.   There is no resisting great good-humour, be what will in the opposite scale.

He entertained us all as if hired for that purpose, telling stories of Dr. Johnson, and acting them with incessant buffoonery.   I told him frankly that if he turned him into ridicule by caricature, I should fly the premises; he assured me he would not, and, indeed, his imitations, though comic to excess, were so far from caricature that he omitted a thousand gesticulations which I distinctly remember.

Mr. Langton told some stories himself in imitation of Dr. Johnson, but they became him less than Mr. Boswell.

I think it would be a mistake to conceive of Boswell's gaiety as a mere flow of animal spirits; he himself would, it is more likely, have called it a "relish of existence."   For "parties of pleasure," as he called meetings designed to stimulate the animal spirits, he had, he insisted, no "ardent love."   He "tasted" experience and association

as a connoisseur tastes old wine.   Perhaps no man
ever lived whose senses were more exquisitely
alive to the manifold joys of social existence.   In
the course of an ill-ordered life he did many a foolish thing: he talked too much about himself, and
babbled of his melancholy to all who listened; he
was vain, and, I fear, he was sensual; moreover,
he was frequently and increasingly drunk.   But
he never insulted his Creator by regarding life as a
dull and uninteresting business.

The consummate proof of Boswell's delight in
social life is of course his abiding habit of recording
it.   He was dissatisfied with mere reminiscence.
He would not trust to his memory, marvelous
though his memory was.   He wanted as full and
accurate an account of life as it was possible to set
down.   One of the most delightful and telling of
his remarks is found near the opening of the "Life
of Johnson," in which he speaks of his desire that
the reader should "live o'er each scene" with
Johnson, that he might as it were "see him live";
and then adds, "Had his other friends been as
diligent and ardent as I was, he might have been
almost completely preserved."

To James Boswell Esqr.

Presented,

as a small, but sincere token
of Love and Esteem,
June 1766.   by W. W.

From Mr William Wallace
Professour of Scots Law.

Inscription in Boswell's copy of Jaussin's "Memoire de la Corse"
the best-known account of Corsica before Boswell's

CHAPTER IX

JOURNAL-KEEPING AND JOURNAL-PUBLISHING

How did Boswell take his notes? Did he take them on the spot, or did he write them up afterwards? Are we to think of him as sitting about the drawing-rooms of the eighteenth century, scratching away like a stenographer? Such questions, I think, the reader of the "Life of Johnson" is always asking himself. They are natural, but are not entirely easy to answer.

In the first place, most of the *prima-facie* evidence is lost. The notes on which the books were based have, in general, perished. In his will Boswell made the following provision for the publication of the materials preserved in the "cabinet" at Auchinleck: "I hereby leave to the said Sir William Forbes, the Reverend Mr. Temple and Edmond Malone, Esquire, all my manuscripts of my own composition, and all my letters from various persons, to be published for the benefit of my younger children, as they shall decide, that is to say, they are to have a discretionary power to publish more or less."

The three executors seem to have lacked interest or initiative. They never met. All that we know

of their rather shocking neglect of duty is derived
from the remarks of the Reverend Dr. Rogers,
one of the earlier biographers of Boswell, who appears to have had access to some private family
information. He says: "The three persons nom-
inated as literary executors did not meet, and the
entire business of the trust was administered by
Sir William Forbes, Bart., who appointed as his
law-agent, Robert Boswell, Writer to the Signet,
cousin-german of the deceased. By that gentleman's advice, Boswell's manuscripts were left to
the disposal of his family; and it is believed that
the whole were immediately destroyed." Com-
ment on such action would be superfluous.

Two of the journals, at least, escaped the flames.
One was the so-called Commonplace Book, from
which quotations have been often drawn in these
essays, and the other was one of the journals used
in the composition of the "Life of Johnson." The
manuscript of the former I have never seen; it is,
perhaps, lost. It was published in 1874, and has
long been familiar to scholars. The original must
have been either a note-book, in which entries were
made at widely-separated intervals, or, perhaps, a
series of loose sheets kept together in a portfolio.
Although the order of the entries is strangely con-
fused, there is some semblance of sequence. The
earliest anecdotes belong to the year 1763, and the

latest date recorded is 1785. It covers, therefore, the most interesting period of Boswell's life.

It is clear that the book was not one of those intended for publication, or even regarded as material to be written up for publication. But it is no less significant and valuable, since it affords us a strictly personal view. It is, in truth, what it has generally been called — a commonplace book, from which, on occasion, the author might draw an anecdote or a *mot*.

The other note-book is of a very different kind. It is, as has been said, one of the journals used in writing the "Life of Johnson." It was filled up at two different periods. In the first place, it contains, set down in chronological order, the facts in Johnson's boyhood and life at Oxford that Boswell had been able to learn from Miss Porter, Johnson's step-daughter, Dr. Adams, Mr. Hector, and others, during a visit to Ashbourne, Lichfield, and Oxford in March, 1776. This entry is continuous and chronological, covering Johnson's life down to his departure for London. An anecdote from Dr. Percy is added; and then, in the month of April, after the return to London, notes on Johnson's relations with Tom Hervey, contributed by Beauclerk, and Langton's account of Johnson's dispute with Dr. Barnard, Dean of Derry. All this, it will be noticed, is material that had been

But the Dean told me at the dinner of the Royal Academicians 22 April 1776 that he had a very great respect for Johnson. I love him said he; but he does not love me & he complained of his rough harsh manners saying that when he smiled ~~he shewed saw~~ the teeth at the corner of his mouth like a dog who is going to bite. He said Johnson is right ninety-nine times in a hundred. I think with him but — You do not feel with him said I. "No, said the Dean. In short he is not a gentleman." The Dean told me he thought of answering his grace & would be glad to talk with Johnson of it. When I came to Bath, Johnson

x that he had been very intimate with... he had been an Author... Sign... never was meant after... recollect; never knew that he ever meant that heritage x

Facsimile of a page from Boswell's Note-book, 1776,
showing material later used in the Life

communicated to Boswell by friends of Johnson. Thus far the note-book is not the record of Johnson's conversation as heard by Boswell. It consists of data which will be of use to Boswell in writing those periods of Johnson's life of which he has not had personal knowledge.

But the most interesting feature of this note-book remains to be mentioned. In September of the following year, Boswell made another visit to Ashbourne, where Johnson was visiting his friend, Dr. Taylor, and carried this same note-book with him, partly in order to correct or amplify what he had recorded in the previous year, and partly to note anything of importance that Johnson might say. When writing in the previous year, he had left half a page blank for future correction; and now, in 1777, he fills up some of this space. In the example reproduced on page 195, the note written lengthwise of the sheet has to do with an earlier page than the one shown in the cut. The correction is so elaborate that it has been continued from page to page.

By a happy chance, Boswell also used this note-book — as he had certainly not originally intended to do — *to record a conversation* which he had with Johnson one evening at Ashbourne; and thus we are provided with one example — the sole surviving one — of the notes which Boswell used for one of the important conversations in the "Life." Because of this unique value, the notes are here reproduced side by side with the corresponding passage, based on them, in the "Life."

NOTE–BOOK

I mentioned the "doom of man," *Unhappiness*, in his "Vanity of human Wishes"; but observed that things were done upon the supposition of happiness. Grand houses were built, fine grardens [*sic*] made. He said these were all ⁺struggles for happiness. He said the first view of Ranelagh gave an expansion and gay sensation to his mind that nothing else had done; but As Xerxes wept to think that n⁰ᵗ one of his great army would be alive years after, he thought that there was not one in the brilliant crowd at Ranelagh that was not afraid to go home and think. The thoughts of each In-

"Life," vol. III, page 198 [1]

I talked to him of misery being "the doom of man" in this life, as displayed in his "Vanity of Human Wishes." Yet I observed that things were done upon the supposition of happiness; grand houses were built, fine gardens were made, splendid places of publick amusement were contrived, and crowded with company.

JOHNSON. "Alas, Sir, these are all only struggles for happiness. When I first entered Ranelagh, it gave an expansion and gay sensation to my mind, such as I never experienced any where else. But, as Xerxes wept when he viewed his immense army,

[1] Birkbeck Hill's edition: Oxford, 1887.

dividual there would be distressing when alone.

and considered that not one of that great multitude would be alive a hundred years afterwards, so it went to my heart to consider that there was not one in all that brilliant circle that was not afraid to go home and think; but that the thoughts of each individual would be distressing when alone."

This reflection was experimentally just. The feeling of languor, which succeeds the animation of gaiety, is itself a very severe pain; and when the mind is then vacant, a thousand disappointments and vexations rush in and excruciate. Will not many even of my fairest readers allow this to be true?

I said that being in love or having some fine project for next day might preserve felicity. He admitted there might be such instances. But in general his conclusion was just. I Myself have never

I suggested, that being in love, and flattered with hopes of success; or having some favourite scheme in view for the next day, might prevent that wretchedness of which we had been talking.

been more miserable than after Ranelagh, when unoccupied & alone in my lodgings, and I suppose almost all the beautiful Ladies whom I have admired there have suffered *then* as I did.

He said he did not imagine that all would be made clear to us immediately after death; but that the ways of Providence would be explained very gradually.

JOHNSON. "Why, Sir, it may sometimes be so as you suppose; but my conclusion is in general but too true."

While Johnson and I stood in calm conference by ourselves in Dr. Taylor's garden, at a pretty late hour in a serene autumn night, looking up to the heavens, I directed the discourse to the subject of a future state. My friend was in a placid and most benignant frame. "Sir, (said he,) I do not imagine that all things will be made clear to us immediately after death, but that the ways of Providence will be explained to us very gradually." I ventured to ask him whether, although the words of some texts of Scripture seemed strong in support of the dreadful doctrine of an eternity of punishment, we might not hope that the denunciation was figurative, and would not literally be executed.

JOHNSON. "Sir, you are to consider the intention of punishment in a future state. We have no reason to be sure that we shall then be no longer liable to offend against GOD. We do not know that even the angels are quite in a state of security; nay, we know that some of them have fallen. It may, therefore, perhaps be necessary, in order to preserve both men and angels in a state of rectitude, that they should have continually before them the punishment of those who have deviated from it; but we may hope that by some other means a fall from rectitude may be prevented. Some of the texts of Scripture upon this subject are, as you observe, indeed strong; but they may admit of a mitigated interpretation."

He talked to me upon

He said he did not know if if [sic] Angels were quite in a state of security. For we know that some of them once fell; but perhaps they were kept in a state of rectitude by having continually before them the punishment of those which deviated; which was the reason for the wicked being eternally punished (if it was so). As to Mankind. I said It was not wrong to hope that it might not be so. He said It was not. We might hope that by some other means, a fall from rectitude might be prevented. I said the words as to everlasting punishment were strong. He said they *were* strong. But

he seemed inclined to miti-gate their interpretation. I was much pleased with this mildness.	this awful and delicate question in a gentle tone, and as if afraid to be decisive.

Here is ample justification of the general confidence that has always been felt in Boswell's accuracy. The passage in the right-hand column is, to be sure, much longer. Boswell has sketched, from memory, the dramatic background, and has put the reader in touch with the circumstances of the conversation; but he has *added* nothing at all except the transition from the ways of Providence to the eternal state of the angels. It is possible that he made up the sentence, "Sir, you are to consider the intention of punishment in a future state"; but, in that case, his creative imagination was assisted by a mind which had become, to use his own phrase, "impregnated with the Johnsonian æther," and it is not likely that, even in this and the following sentence, he is far from the *ipsissima verba* of Johnson. The passage may confidently be taken as typical of Boswell's regular method of dealing with his journals.

But meanwhile we are leaving unanswered the question that was originally proposed: How did Boswell make his note-books? In general, he wrote up his records in the first convenient interval after the conversation had taken place, depending on his memory for the general scope and order of the remarks. *In certain exceptional cases*, he appears to have jotted down notes on the spot. There are two passages in the "Tour to Corsica" which probably give us as accurate a notion of his general procedure as we are likely ever to get.

From my first setting out on this tour, I wrote down every night what I had observed during the day, throwing together a great deal, that I might afterwards make a selection at leisure. . . .
I regret that the fire with which he spoke upon such occasions so dazzled me that I could not recollect his sayings so as to write them down when I retired from his presence.

To this should be added the amazing evidence given in the first volume of the "Life," in reference to the spring of 1763, when Boswell was twenty-two years old.

We staid so long at Greenwich, that our sail up the river, in our return to London, was by no means so pleasant as in the morning; for the night air was so cold that it made me shiver. I was the more sensible of it from having sat up all the night before, recollecting and writing in my journal what I thought worthy of preservation; an exertion, which, during the first part of my acquaintance with Johnson, I frequently made. I remember having sat up four nights in one week, without being much incommoded in the daytime.

On the other hand, we are to remember that
Paoli thought at first that Boswell was a spy because the young man was "to the work of writing down all that he said." Mrs. Thrale, when
she wrote her "Anecdotes of Johnson," sneered at
Boswell's trick "of sitting steadily down at the
other end of the room to write at the moment what
should be said in company." To which he replied
in the "Life" : —

She has, in flippant terms enough, expressed her disapprobation of that anxious desire of authenticity
which prompts a person who is to record conversations
to write them down *at the moment*. Unquestionably,
if they are to be recorded at all, the sooner it is done the
better.

These two are the chief passages on which a
comparison of Boswell to a stenographer can be
based; and we are to remember that it is a kind
of evidence which people are likely to exaggerate,
in their desire to find proof of a notion which has
already been formed in their mind. It would certainly be a most serious error to think of Boswell
as recording any large amount of his conversa-
tional material "at the moment." The bulk of it
unquestionably was written down in private, as he
himself has told us was his habit. The note-book
which we have been examining supports this view,

as I have tried to show; and so does the well-known anecdote in the "Life," in which, during a particularly brilliant conversation of Johnson's, Boswell remarked to Mrs. Thrale, "O for short-hand to take this down" and she replied, "You 'll carry it all in your head. A long head is as good as short hand."

If the fact that he did most of his writing after the event tends to make anyone doubt the accuracy of his record, it is because he has failed to reckon with the fidelity of the man's memory. It is to be recalled that Boswell began keeping a journal before he was eighteen years old, and, so far as we know, never interrupted the practice. He was constantly engaged in recording conversations that he had heard, and the resultant training of his literal memory we are not likely to exaggerate. Most of us have no memory of conversation, for two very simple reasons. In the first place, we have no great desire to preserve it; and, secondly, we have never tried writing it down. It is prob-able that a training of two weeks in such a practice would enable a man to make a fairly faithful rec-ord of conversation. In Boswell's case that train-ing was extended over the whole of his maturity, called forth all the power that was in him, and was regarded by himself as his most precious faculty. He knew his journals as a musician knows his score, or a lover his mistress. When he was engaged in reading the proof-sheets of the "Life," he altered a statement that he had set down about the conversation of Edmund Burke. In the proofs Johnson is quoted as remarking, "His vigour of mind is incessant"; but Boswell has corrected this to read, "His stream of mind is perpetual"; and adds (as an explanation to the proof-reader): "I restore. I find the exact words as to Burke." What happened is, I think, clear. Boswell had lost the original record, and had reconstructed the remark about Burke from memory, using such words as he imagined Johnson to have employed; but, in the course of his labours on the proofs, he discovered the original entry in some one of his numerous note-books.[1]

In view of this meticulous carefulness, it is not surprising that he boasted of the "scrupulous fidelity" of his journal. He knew the value of what he was doing. He knew that his journals were, even in their undeveloped form, very near to the level of literature. In his Commonplace

[1] The two little sentences are worth a moment's study, because they show the quality of Johnson's conversation which it was hardest to imitate — his imagery. It is clear that Boswell has preserved in memory the significance of what Johnson had said about Burke, but the flavour — the "bouquet" of the remark, if I may use the expression — is lost with the metaphor.

Book he records, *à propos* of nothing, the following
sentence : "My journal is ready ; it is in the larder,
only to be sent to the kitchen, or perhaps trussed
and larded a little." He had no intention of wast-
ing the contents of his larder. He had proved the
value of his wares, while still a young man, with
his "Account of Corsica." The portion of the
book which had been praised by everyone was the
journal of his personal experiences and conversations with Paoli, the part which is commonly referred to by the separate title of the "Tour to
Corsica." He had found his vein of genius. It
ran in the direction of personal reminiscence, not
in the direction of history. He had kept records
of all his experiences on the Continent, and had
planned some time or other to publish them, in-
cluding the conversations which he had held there
with the Great.

This plan was never realised ; but a more remarkable experience than any which had befallen
him upon the Continent awaited him in his own
country. In August, 1773, his long-cherished plan
of visiting the Highlands and the Hebrides in
company with Dr. Johnson was carried out. They
left Edinburgh on the eighteenth of the month,
consumed almost two months and a half in travel,
and arrived at Auchinleck, on their return, on

the second day of November. Throughout this trip Boswell employed all his ingenuity and brought into play all the varied influence which the son of Lord Auchinleck could exert in Scotland, in order to give the Great Lexicographer a good time. Their journey was a royal progress, save that they were spared that boredom which royalty must endure. Their trip was thorough and complete, and they returned without any vain regrets. They had seen everything worth seeing, and had met everybody worth meeting. They had had a great deal of pure fun, and acquired a store of information. And Johnson owed all this to Boswell. Perhaps no man ever exerted himself more continuously or ingeniously to pleasure a friend on his travels. Boswell's hope was that Johnson would write a book about it. Of course, he himself kept a journal of everything they had seen and everything Johnson had said.

There was one aspect of the journey that had a special importance in Boswell's eyes. Johnson was, in a sense, in the "enemy's country." As has been remarked by critics, with wearisome iteration, his dislike of Scotland and the Scots was a harmless and amusing affectation; but he had played the rôle so long that the public would not let him drop it, even had he been so disposed. When it was known that Johnson was to visit

Scotland, his friends were convulsed with mirth.
It was as if an anti-Semite were to propose to go
and disport himself in Jewry. There was no
doubt that the public would buy and read any book
on Scotland which he might publish. Boswell
knew both his country and his friend too well to
fear that any real injustice would be done to a
great and good people. His apprehension was of
a quite different kind. He feared that Johnson
might never bring himself to write the book. Johnson was known to be lazy. Something must be
done about it.

Johnson left Scotland on the twenty-second of
November, and Boswell accompanied him as far
as Blackshields, fourteen miles on the road from
Edinburgh to London. There they passed the
night at an inn. The next morning Boswell saw
his venerable companion safe into the fly for New-
castle. On the same day he addressed a letter to
Henry Thrale, which begins as follows : —

I had the pleasure to receive a few lines from you
in August when you enclosed a letter to Mr. Johnson
under cover to me. Since that time our much-respected
friend and I have had a long and very curious tour,
of which his letters have, I suppose, given you and
Mrs. Thrale a pretty full account. The world, however, I hope, will have a still fuller account from him.
I hope you and Mrs. Thrale will not be wanting in

keeping [him] in mind of the expectations which he has raised. . . . I flatter myself that he shall have no cause to repent of his northern expedition.

The ostensible reason for writing this letter to Thrale was to forward a letter to Miss Anna Williams, Johnson's blind housekeeper, which he had forgotten to send by Johnson; but the vital purpose is visible to him who runs. Boswell would not lose a day before he began the application of that stimulus which was necessary if the world was ever to get the story of Johnson's journey to the western islands of Scotland. Throughout the winter, therefore, he continued to keep Johnson mindful of his original plan, for he well knew the great man's capacity for forgetting a definite literary task. In response to a question which Johnson asked him about the order of the clans, he wrote: "I like your little memorandums; they are symptoms of your being in earnest with your book of northern travels." As late as the next April he wrote to David Garrick: "I hope Mr. Johnson has given you an entertaining account of his northern tour. He is certainly to favour the world with some of his remarks. Pray do not fail to quicken him by word, as I do by letter."

All this goading was not administered merely for the glory of Samuel Johnson, or the vindication of Scotland. There was certainly some thought of the reputation which Boswell would acquire as the projector of the entire expedition and the chosen companion of the author. When the book appeared, he found a pleasant reference to himself in the first paragraph, as a "companion whose acuteness would help his inquiry, and whose gaiety of conversation and civility of manners are sufficient to counteract the inconveniencies of travel in countries less hospitable than we have passed."

This was gratifying, of course; but the book as a whole failed to satisfy Boswell. He had had the highest expectations. "He is certainly to give the world some account of his tour to the Highlands and Hebrides," he had written to Langton before the publication of the book; "he will not only entertain more richly than an ordinary traveller, but will furnish instruction on a variety of subjects." And so indeed he did, for the "Journey to the Western Islands of Scotland" is a fine performance. But it may be doubted whether a book produced at the instigation of another is ever quite satisfactory to its "only begetter." When the book appeared, Boswell at once wrote to Johnson in its praise: "The more I read your *Journey*, the more satisfaction I receive. . . . I can hardly conceive how, in so short a time, you acquired the knowledge of so many particulars." And yet that knowledge was not perfect. A native Scot, with a keen eye and a well-stored journal of his own, could detect in the book a multitude of minor errors, and, what was more important, a number of lost opportunities to entertain the general reader. He, therefore, with a *naïveté* characteristic of him, as if the mere truth were the only matter to be considered, sat down and wrote out a series of "Remarks on the Journey to the Western Islands of Scotland," in which he not only pointed out errors, but made suggestions here and there respecting the improvement of the diction. His comments are too extensive to be reprinted entire; the following specimens may serve as typical.

P. 256, at the bottom. Is it right to change the tense? "*is* labouring" . . . "*arose.*"

Your reflections on Highland learning, on the Bards, and on Ossian amount to *Demonstration;* only on page 274 *if any can be found* might have been omitted; for I take it to be certain that *some* wandering Ballads are inserted in *Fingal.* And on page 275, you are mistaken in telling "it was never said that any of them could recite *six lines.*" Some of them do actually recite many more.

P. 277, 1. 13. A triffling inaccuracy. We did not leave *Sky* in a boat that was taking in kelp. It was a boat from Ilay, in which a Gentleman had come in quest of an emigrant who owed him money. But before he came the emigrant was sailed. On the same page you treat the storm too lightly. Col and all the islanders thought we were really in danger.

I observe you sometimes write *Erse* and sometimes *Earse ;* one or other only must be right.

P. 286, 1. 8, for Brecacig — Breacachach.

P. 296 (erroneously printed 226). This page I believe will make me yet go to the popish islands. But I must have instructions from you in writing.

Of the reception of this document by the Sage we have no account, but it may safely be left to the reader's imagination. Boswell ultimately went so far as to propose to publish a sort of supplement to the "Journey"; but, after his trip to London in the spring of 1775, this amazing plan was, happily, dropped. In May he wrote to Temple : —

I have not written out another line of my "Remarks on the Hebrides." I found it impossible to do it in London. Besides, Dr. Johnson does not seem very desirous that I should publish any supplement. Between ourselves, he is not apt to encourage one to *share* reputation with himself. But don't you think I may write out my remarks in Scotland, and send them to be revised by you, and then they may be published freely?

Such was the origin of the "Journal of a Tour to the Hebrides with Samuel Johnson, LL.D.," perhaps the sprightliest book of travels in the language. A decade was to elapse, and Johnson to pass away, ere the publication of the book; but Boswell had his reward for fulfilling the Horatian

principle of delay.   The lapse of time enabled him
to publish, not a supplement to Johnson's book,
but an independent volume, in which he was not
to "share" Johnson's fame as a writer of travels,
but totally to eclipse it.   Moreover, the death of
his eminent companion enabled him to cast all

Johnson, the Bear, with Boswell, in Scotland
From a contemporary caricature

restraint aside and to print, as literally as he chose
to do, the diary which he had kept during the tour.
Of this diary and of the "Tour to the Hebrides"
he speaks in identical terms.   Once only (under
date of September 4) does he speak of suppressing
material in the diary.

This diary had, as it were, the approval —
though by no means the *imprimatur* — of Samuel

Johnson.   He was well acquainted with Boswell's journal-keeping habits, and had often seen him at work upon it.   After reading it, he made the remark that it was a very exact picture of a portion of his life.   We have Boswell's word for it that Johnson was also aware of his intention to produce a biography of him.   And yet to assert all this is not to say that Johnson ever conceived of the possibility of Boswell's printing the journal as it stood.   Print the journal!   He would as soon have permitted Reynolds to paint him in a state of nature.

When, in 1785, the "Tour" appeared, Johnson had been in his grave nearly a twelvemonth; but though he was not alive, to protest in person, his friends protested for him.   Nothing like it had ever been read.   It became at once a standard of indiscretion.   To compare it with the autobiographical revelations made, in our own day, by the wife of a former Prime Minister of Great Britain would be to adduce but a feeble parallel.   Boswell calmly recorded Johnson's casual remarks about everybody he had met.   Lord Errol, for example, was told that the pillows on his bed had a disagreeable smell.   Lord Monboddo was still alive, to read Johnson's contemptuous opinion of his theory of man's descent from monkeys, and was told that he was "as jealous of his tail as a squirrel." He might also read that Johnson disapproved of his round hat, and considered him a fool for calling himself "Farmer Burnet." The Macaulay family were informed that Johnson said he did not believe that the Reverend Kenneth Macaulay (or M'Auley) of Calder was capable of writing the "History of St. Kilda's" which had appeared under his name — a slight which Trevelyan, writing nearly a century later, still found it impossible to pardon. The insult to Sir Alexander McDonald ("I meditated an escape from this house the very next day; but Dr. Johnson resolved that we should weather it out till Monday") and that to the famous Duchess of Hamilton are too well known to need repetition. When Rowlandson and Collings published their popular series of caricatures of the "Tour," one plate represented Boswell as "revising for a second edition," while Sir Alexander, brandishing a stick, stands over him as he tears out certain pages of the book. In the second edition Boswell did, indeed, make certain alterations in the interests of discretion, and spoke of a "few observations" which "might be considered as passing the bounds of a strict decorum"; but enough remained to require the revision of every principle of decorum of which the eighteenth century had ever conceived.

In October, a friend of Bishop Percy's wrote to

him about the book, remarking, "I have been amused at it, but should be very sorry either to have been the author or the hero of it." A pamphlet in the form of a letter to Boswell was written by a penny-a-liner calling himself "Verax," in which he said: "You have forced upon the Public a six-shilling book replete with small talk and ill-natured remarks." This wretched hack professed to fear that the public would soon "have volume upon volume of coffee-house chit-chat or amorous *tête-à-têtes*." A satire, entitled "A Poetical Epistle from the Ghost of Dr. Johnson to his Friends," contains the following lines: —

> O ne'er shall I our curious jaunt forget;
> When, hungry, cold, sleepy, fatigu'd and wet,
> On musty hay we vainly sought repose. . . .
> How oft I mark'd thee, like a watchful cat,
> List'ning to catch up all my silly chat;
> How oft that chat I still more silly made,
> To see it in thy common-place conveyed!

So much for the attack of Boswell's enemies. But his friends were scarcely less of a burden to him. He was deluged with a Niagara of advice, urging him to be more cautious. One page, in particular, roused the dismay of everyone who had known Johnson. This was the sheet of advertisement at the end, in which Boswell announced to the public that he was at work upon a biography of Johnson, that he had been collecting

" *Revising for the Second Edition* "

From Rowlandson and Collings's Series of Caricatures of the *Tour to the Hebrides* (1786)

The author of the *Tour*, threatened by Sir Alexander McDonald

materials for twenty years, and that the book would include "several curious particulars," as well as "the most authentick accounts that can be obtained from those who knew him best."

Johnson's acquaintances were seized with alarm. What would be their fate in the new book? If Boswell had created so great a disturbance in Scotland by his account of three months in Johnson's life, what would be the result in England when he published a history of the whole seventy-five years of it? Fanny Burney, as we have seen, refused her assistance, and wrote in her "Diary": "I feel sorry to be named or remembered by that biographical, anecdotical memorandummer till his book of poor Dr. Johnson's life is finished and published." One of his best friends, Sir William Forbes, who was later to be appointed one of his literary executors, took umbrage at the fact that Boswell had quoted his approval of the journal, before it was in print, and took the liberty of "strongly enjoining him" to be more careful about personalities in the later work.

But Boswell was not dismayed. He had the solid satisfaction of seeing two large editions of the "Tour" devoured by the eager public. He might, indeed, have gone too far in certain instances. He answered his critics, in the second edition, by charging them with a failure to understand the true motive of his recording anecdotes which were sometimes to his own disadvantage, the objections to which he saw as clearly as did they. "But it would be an endless task," he continued, "for an authour to point out upon every occasion the precise object he has in view. Contenting himself with the approbation of readers of discernment and taste, he ought not to complain that some are found who cannot or will not understand him."

It may be doubted whether such attacks as Boswell suffered ever really injure a book. The indiscretions which shocked the nerves of the eighteenth century have lost something of their tang in the passage of the years; but the naïve charm of the book remains. More than any work of Boswell's it preserves the freshness and authenticity of his journals. If one of the objects of literature be to mirror human association and companionship when at their fullest and most zestful, then this book must ever be accorded a very high rank. It has a unity and an intimacy denied even to the great "Life of Johnson"; for the geographical isolation of the Hebrides, and the limitation of the account to a single period in the life of the man recorded, render it, if possible, a more vivid book than the biography, which is, inevitably, more diffuse. Moreover, it has the advantage of de-

picting Johnson in an unusual environment, likely
to stimulate his powers of observation and lend
point and colour to his remarks.   It tells the story
of a long holiday; and it has, therefore, the mirth
and abandon of spirit characteristic of two friends
whose chief aim, at the moment, is to have a good
time.   All that is most likable in Boswell appears,
and all that is depressing — his melancholy, for
instance — takes flight from its cheerful pages.
It is the happiest of books, and it has lost none of
its original power of rendering its readers happy,
too.

CHAPTER X

THE MAGNUM OPUS

THERE is a certain kind of reader who vexes himself and teases the critic with the question whether the author of a great classic really put into it all that an enthusiastic reader asserts that he finds. Is it a conscious art, or has all the greatness, all the subtlety and meaning of it, been thrust upon it by the critic? A suspicious reader can usually be set right by passages in which the author himself has spoken of his art. A critic is as little likely to see more than he was intended to see as a stream is likely to rise above its source. If anybody doubts whether Boswell meant to produce the effects for which he is famous, let him gather up everything that the man said about his art, about Johnson's theory of biography, and, above all, everything that he said about his own books, and he will convince himself that Boswell's effects were all calculated.

I have analysed elsewhere the characteristics which, in my opinion, distinguish the "Life of Johnson," and account for the supreme position to which it has been universally assigned. That analysis I do not propose to repeat. It may suffice to say that Boswell's general notion was to defy the very powers of oblivion and to preserve his friend as complete and as vivid as he had been in the flesh. With a sufficient amount of assiduity from a sufficient number of people, such a result, he thought, might almost have been attained. Perhaps he was right. Perhaps, on the other hand, he failed to reckon with the fact that not everyone who might feel inclined to record Dr. Johnson had the genius of a Boswell for doing it.

In all Boswell's complacent references to himself, in the whole range of his pomposity and self-conceit, he never once called himself that which in fullest truth he was — a genius. I doubt whether Boswell ever guessed that he was a genius. His fault was vanity — conceit, if you will — rather than pride. I mean that he loved to talk about himself, loved to dream of becoming a "great man," strutted and put on airs, but never, so far as I am aware, really overestimated his own powers or his own achievement. He was modest in his own despite, though having no intention whatever of being so. In the group of quotations about the "Life of Johnson" that follow, there is much vanity, and a great deal more of self-assertion than there should be; but there is nothing in all his references to himself that can for a moment compare with Macaulay's famous summary, to

which, I fancy, every critic would now assent:
"Homer is not more decidedly the first of heroic
poets, Shakespeare is not more decidedly the first
of dramatists, Demosthenes is not more decidedly
the first of orators, than Boswell is the first of biographers. He has no second. He has distanced
all his competitors so decidedly that it is not worth
while to place them. Eclipse is first, and the rest
nowhere." And again, "He has, in an important
department of literature, immeasurably surpassed
such writers as Tacitus, Clarendon, Alfieri, and his
own idol Johnson." Had Boswell read such sentences as these about himself he would have
swooned with amazement.

The three passages which I here adduce were all
written in the early months of the year 1788. The
first is from a letter to Bishop Percy, thanking him
for the assistance which he had given.

Procrastination, we all know, increases in a propor-
tionate ratio the difficulty of doing that which might
have once been done very easily. I am really uneasy to
think how long it is since I was favoured with your
Lordship's communications concerning Dr. Johnson,
which, though few, are valuable, and will contribute
to increase my store. I am ashamed that I have yet
seven years to write of his life. I do it chronologically,
giving year by year his publications, if there were any;
his letters, his conversations, and every thing else that
I can collect. It appears to me that mine is the best

plan of biography that can be conceived; for my readers
will, as near as may be, accompany Johnson in his
progress, and, as it were, see each scene as it happened.
I am of opinion that my delay will be for the advantage of the work, though perhaps not for the advantage
of the author, both because his fame may suffer from
too great expectation, and the sale may be worse from
the subject being comparatively old.   But I mean to do
my duty as well as I can.

Some six weeks later he wrote to Temple : —

Mason's "Life of Gray" is excellent, because it is
interspersed with letters which show us the *Man*.   His
"Life of Whitehead" is not a Life at all; for there is
neither a letter nor a saying from first to last.   I am
absolutely certain that *my* mode of biography, which
gives not only a *history* of Johnson's *visible* progress
through the world, and of his publications, but a *view*
of his mind, in his letters and conversations, is the most
perfect that can be conceived, and will be *more* of a *Life*
than any work that has ever yet appeared.

In April he wrote to Miss Anna Seward (the
"Swan of Lichfield"), in reference to the various
works on Johnson that had appeared : Hawkins's
"Life," Mrs. Thrale's "Anecdotes," her "Letters
of Samuel Johnson," Tyers's biographical sketch,
Towers's essay, "Last Words of Samuel Johnson,"
and "More Last Words" : —

What a variety of publications have there been concerning Johnson.   Never was there a man whose repu-

tation remained so long in such luxuriant freshness as his does. How very envious of this do the "little stars" of literature seem to be, though bright themselves in their due proportion. My Life of that illustrious man has been retarded by several avocations, as well as by depression of mind. But I hope to have it ready for the press next month. I flatter myself it will exhibit him more completely than any person, ancient or modern, has yet been preserved, and whatever merit I may be allowed, the world will at least owe to my assiduity the possession of a rich intellectual treasure.

It will be seen from the last sentence that Boswell made a distinction in his own mind between the importance of the principles which he had discovered and the particular biography which he had written; and in drawing this distinction the present writer may hope to avoid the charge of inconsistency. Boswell had full confidence in the method which he had adopted, and counted on it to help him write "more of a Life than any that has ever yet appeared"; but that he had not only found the method but also written the classic example of it, — that he was, to speak temperately, as illustrious a writer as Johnson, — this, luckily, he did not see. Plainly, it is of his "assiduity" rather than his genius that he boasts.

To Boswell, I suppose, the task seemed to make a special demand upon one's assiduity. The work

The Biographers

(Mrs. Piozzi, John Courtenay, Boswell)

Beneath the engraving in the original, dated "Jan. 1786, J. Cornell, Bruton Street," appears the following travesty of Dryden's famous lines under a portrait of Milton:

Three Authors in three Sister Kingdoms born
The Shrine of Johnson with their Works adorn.
The first a female Friend with letter'd Pride
Bares those Defects which Friendship ought to hide.
B——ll to Genius gives a Monster's Air
And shews his Johnson as Men shew a Bear.
C——y to Merit as to Grammar true,
Blurs with bad Verse the worth he never knew.
O could the Sage whose Fame employs their Pen
Visit his great Biographers again,
His two good Friends would find him d——d uncivil,
And he would drive the Poet to the Devil.

that had required genius (which, let me add, is a
great deal more than an infinite capacity for
taking pains) was over and done with. Boswell's
genius, as distinct from mere industry, had exhibited itself in originating such a plan and in the
whole conception of Johnson as the hero of a drama
of almost national proportions; in his realisation
of the importance and interest of Johnson's talk,
and in getting it on paper. He was annoyed, as
every author is, by the people who were afraid
of him, afraid that he "might put them in a book."
People hesitated to meet him after the publication
of the "Life," and wondered whether their every
word would be written down by this deputy of the
Recording Angel. He had something like a quarrel
with his friend, Sir William Scott, because that
gentleman, in inviting him to dine, had seen fit to
caution him not to embarrass the guests by writing
down their conversation. Boswell thereupon declined the invitation. Sir William wrote to him,
explaining the "principle" of his request, and
apparently pointed out that the persons who
feared to meet Boswell were thinking of the lot of
the minor characters in the "Life," who had
served only as foils to Johnson. Boswell, in accepting the apology, made the following declara-
tion of his own principles, which, it will be seen,
was intended as a sort of official utterance.

If others, as well as myself, sometimes appear as shades to the Great Intellectual Light, I beg to be fairly understood, and that you and my other friends will inculcate upon persons of timidity and reserve, that my recording the conversation of so extraordinary a man as Johnson, with its concomitant circumstances, was a *peculiar* undertaking, attended with much anxiety and labour, and that the conversations of people in general are by no means of that nature as to bear being registered, and that the task of doing it would be exceedingly irksome to me. Ask me, then, my dear Sir, with none but who are clear of a prejudice which you see may easily be cured. I trust there are enough who have it not.

It is clear from this that Boswell deemed himself more than a mere realist who was registering life just as it is. It was not sufficient to make records. It was essential first to find your "great intellectual light." That was the work of genius, as it was the work of genius to conceive the tremendous plan of letting the reader accompany Johnson on his "progress through life."

But the task of taking infinite pains remained. Boswell was almost submerged by his own material, not to speak of the material, good and bad, that poured in upon him, every scrap of which must be tested for its authenticity as well as for its inherent interest. The marvel is that he did not

give up the task. Indeed, the thought occurred
to him, for he wrote to Temple : —

You cannot imagine what labour, what perplexity,
what vexation, I have endured in arranging a prodi-
gious multiplicity of materials, in supplying omissions,
in searching for papers buried in different masses —
and all this besides the exertion of composing and
polishing. Many a time have I thought of giving it up.
However, though I shall be uneasily sensible of its
many deficiencies, it will certainly be to the world a very
valuable and peculiar volume of biography, full of literary and characteristical anecdotes (which word, by
the way, Johnson always condemned as used in the
sense that the French, and we from them, use it, as
signifying *particulars*), told with authenticity and in a
lively manner. Would that it were in the booksellers'
shops. Methinks, if I had this *Magnum Opus*
launched, the publick has no farther claim upon me.

One of the evidences of the greatness of the book
is the fact that so little has, in the course of a hundred and thirty years, been added to our information about Johnson. If we except Miss Burney's
"Diary," which Boswell tried in vain to tap, no
record of first-rate interest and no really novel view
of Johnson have been discovered. Dr. Hill published two volumes of "Johnsonian Miscellanies,"
uniform with the "Life," which, if they serve no
other purpose, cause the work of Boswell to shine
by contrast. Every scrap about Johnson has been

gathered up and given to the world, — I have myself taken part in the work, — and the world has
quite properly neglected it, preferring Boswell.

Immediately after the appearance of the "Tour"
Boswell began his preparations for writing the
"Life." His first task was to collect Johnson's
letters and such reminiscences of him as seemed
authentic. He made application by letter to
Bishop Percy, the Reverend Dr. Adams of Oxford,
Francis Barber (who had in his possession papers
of the highest value to a biographer of Johnson),
Anna Seward, and, no doubt, to a score of others.
The material which he received from such con-
tributors he often wrote down in their presence,
or revised the written record in their presence. It
is to be regretted that we have no account of any
of these sessions, for they would have revealed
the biographer at one of his most characteristic and
important tasks, which must have exercised all the
powers of insinuation and tact which he possessed.
He thought at first that he could finish the book
by the spring of 1789; but the care of Auchinleck,
the death of Mrs. Boswell in the early summer,
and his ill-advised candidacy at the General Election for an *ad interim* membership in Parliament,
conspired to prevent it. Moreover there was his
"master," Lord Lonsdale, upon whom it was neces-

sary to dance attendance and who frequently summoned Boswell to his table to provide amusement (of no literary kind) for his retainers or "Ninepins."

Yet, in spite of all interruptions, he had nearly completed the first draft before the year was out, and by February, 1790, he could say that it was fairly in the press. The printers of the eighteenth century were a long-suffering generation. They actually began the printing of a book before the author had completed the manuscript. When they had received enough copy to fill up a sheet, the type was set, and proofs were pulled and sent to the author for correction. When he returned them, the sheet was printed and folded, and the type in the form distributed. The printer's devil hovered between the compositors and the author, bearing proofs hot from the press and appeals for more copy. It is only by imagining such a state of affairs, alien enough from those of our day, that we can understand the circumstances of Boswell's life in 1790 and 1791, when his "great work" was passing through the press before he himself had completed the rough draft of it. He gasped sometimes at its ever-increasing magnitude, and baulked at first at the thought of two volumes.

His chief assistant in the work — a man who has never received his due for his generous and friendly service — was Edmond Malone, the Shakespearean scholar. Malone, as a member of the Literary Club, had known Johnson. He respected Boswell's genius. The friendship of the two men is said, by a somewhat doubtful anecdote, to have been cemented (if not actually formed) in 1785, in the printing-house, where Boswell found Malone examining with admiration one of the proof-sheets of the "Tour to the Hebrides." Malone's labours on the "Life" began with the revision of the rough draft of the manuscript, which Boswell read aloud to him in the quiet of Malone's "elegant study." Of the copy that was sent to the printer no sheet is known to exist; but we have two sets of proof-sheets, both of which were scanned, in whole or in part, by Malone.

These proof-sheets are a fascinating study. Their owner, Mr. R. B. Adam (a Johnsonian scholar of no mean standing) has repeatedly provided me with opportunities for examining them. The first of the two sets covers only 224 pages of the first volume,[1] of which three signatures (I, K, and L) are lacking. The set consists exclusively of the sheets for which Boswell had demanded a second "revise," or corrected proof; so that the lack of the three signatures may merely indicate that, in these cases, no revision was asked for —

[1] The references are to the first edition of the *Life*, London, 1791.

Edmond Malone

Engraving by J. Scott, from a portrait by Sir Joshua Reynolds

This famous Shakespearean commentator, a member of the Literary Club, rendered
Boswell invaluable aid in preparing the manuscript and reading the proofs of the
Life, of which he annotated four later editions

that is to say, that Boswell had but one proof of
those particular sheets. This entire set of proof-
sheets is quite new to the world of scholars, though
it may have been known to "collectors" in England. Mr. Adam acquired it in March, 1920.

The other set of proof-sheets, bought for £127
by the elder Adam in 1893, is practically complete.
These proofs were sold when the Auchinleck
library was, in part, dispersed; they passed from
the hands of the salesmen, Messrs. Sotheby, Wilkinson and Hodge, to Mr. Adam, who added them
to his already famous collection of Johnsoniana
and Boswelliana in Buffalo. There they were
examined by the great editor of the "Life," Dr.
George Birkbeck Hill, whose study of them may
be found in the first volume of "Johnson Club
Papers," published by Mr. Fisher Unwin in 1899.
This set of proof-sheets also lacks one or two signatures, — why, I do not know, — the loss of
which has been made good by the insertion of the
corresponding pages from the first edition.

Whether still other proof-sheets may be found,
it is difficult to say. Certainly there was never
more than one *complete* set. One or two more of
the earlier sets of "revises" will probably turn up;
but there is, I think, no great doubt that Mr.
Adam's library now contains most of the proof-
sheets that ever existed. It is probable that, as

Boswell progressed in his work, not more than one proof was necessary. One sheet in the set, marked as approved for the printer, bears the message in the compositor's or "corrector's" hand, "More copy, please" — a plain indication that only one proof was then being shown.

Apart from merely verbal changes in the interests of style, the important alterations in these proof-sheets are of two kinds: (1) insertion of new matter in the text; and (2) excision of "old" matter, already set up in type. Of these the latter is by far the more important. We are not specially interested to know when a given paragraph or sentence was introduced into the work; whereas a suppressed passage may — nay, probably does — contain information more piquant than that of the context, and may give us new facts. For example, it is not significant to know that the paragraph about Johnson's faith in the supernatural [1] was an insertion after the printing had begun; but it is interesting to read Boswell's opinion of Goldsmith's attire, which was first inserted, and then struck out: "His dress [was] unsuitably gawdy and without taste." In writing of Mr. Wedderburn's Scotch dialect, it is first said, "Though his voice produce not a silver tone, but rather a hard *iron sound*, if that expression

[1] *Life*, first edition, vol. 1, p. 219.

may be used." This remark Boswell struck out of the proof as, presumably, too personal.

But, in general, the excisions are remarkably few. The additions are much more numerous, and are usually put in to lend colour and variety. For example, when Dr. Adams suggested to Johnson that he engage, as assistant in a projected task, the French Dr. Maty, Boswell wrote, at first:

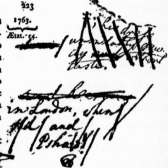

"Johnson declared his disapprobation of this in contemptuous tones"; but altered it to read: "'He' (said Johnson), 'the little black dog! I'd throw him into the Thames.'" Here evidently was a remark which Boswell decided, on second thoughts, it was safe to risk. So, again, the illustrations of odd definitions in Johnson's Dictionary were added in the first proof.

The writing on the proof-sheets is in at least four different hands. Boswell's own comments are

I am much pleased with this sheet as now arranged. As I have made a little alteration which will only shorten a note a line or so, let me have another Revise sent to Sir Joshua Reynolds in Leicester Square where I dine, & it shall be returned instantly

THE

LIFE

OF

SAMUEL JOHNSON, LL.D.

TO write the life of him who excelled all mankind in writing the lives of others, and who, whether we consider his extraordinary endowments, or his various works, has been equalled by few in any age, is an arduous, and may be reckoned in me a presumptuous task.

Had Dr. Johnson written his own life, in conformity with the opinion which he has given[1], that every man's life may be best written by himself; had he employed in the preservation of his own history, that clearness of narration and elegance of language in which he has embalmed so many eminent persons, the world would probably have had the most perfect example of biography that was ever exhibited. But although he at different times, in a desultory manner, committed to writing many particulars of the progress of his mind and fortunes, he never had persevering diligence enough to form them into a regular composition. Of these memorials a few have been preserved; but the greater part was consigned by him to the flames, a few days before his death.

As I had the honour and happiness of enjoying his friendship for upwards of twenty years; as I had the scheme of writing his life constantly in view; as he was well apprised of this circumstance, and from time to time obligingly satisfied my inquiries, by communicating to me the incidents of his early years; as I acquired a facility in recollecting, and was very assiduous in

[1] Idler, No. 84.

B

recording

Proof-sheet of the " Life," first revise

paſſage here and there, have agreed that they could not help going
through, and bcing entertained through the whole. I wiſh, indeed,
ſome few groſs expreſſions had been ſoftened, and a few of our hero's
foibles had been a little more ſhaded; but it is uſeful to ſee the weak-
neſſes incident to great minds; and you have given us Dr. Johnſon's
authority that in hiſtory all ought to be told."

nor will I conceal my ſatisfaction in the And I feel

Such a ſanction to my faculty of giving a juſt repreſentation of Dr.
Johnſon I could not conceal

I am fully perſuaded

that by preſerving recording ſo conſiderable a portion of the wisdom and wit of the brightest ornament of the eighteenth century I have largely provided for the instruction and entertainment of Mankind.

London 20 April 1791.

ALPHABETICAL

Note See Mr Malone's Preface to his Edition of Shakspeare.
Sir There is a date in the Dedication — would you wish to have one here?

Proof-sheet of the " Life " : last page of the " Advertisement,"
or Preface, first revise

not infrequently of that highly personal character which distinguishes whatever he did — " Let me have another *Revise* sent to Sir Joshua Reynolds's in Liecester [*sic*] Square, where I dine, and it shall be returned *instantly*." "I am sorry the compositor has so much trouble." "I shall see this at the Printing house to-morrow morning before it is thrown off. Tuesday." "This Remains till an answer comes from Dr. Warton." Few books have been read for the printer with more scrupulous care.

Malone saw the proof-sheets of three quarters of the book. His advice was generally intended to make the style smoother. For example, on page 84, he writes of Johnson's poem, "Friendship," which Boswell had introduced without sufficient explanation, "Something sh^d be s^d about its appearing in this year & having been given by Mr. Hector." On page 124, he comments, "Too abrupt"; and adds a sentence of his own, to serve as introduction to Dr. Johnson's letter to Birch. By an odd error Dr. Birkbeck Hill assumed that Malone's handwriting was that of the "corrector" at the printing-house, and thus he missed the significance of some of the corrections. It was Malone, for example, who suggested to Boswell that he should suppress the mention of Johnson's hands as "not over-clean," in the famous scene which depicts Johnson as squeezing lemons into a

punch-bowl, and calling out, "Who's for *poonsh* ?"
"'He must have been a stout man,' said Garrick,
'who would have been for it.'" This remark, too,
was cancelled at the same time.

Five of the signatures (or folded sheets of eight
pages) are marked by Malone as approved for the
press. These are Rr – Xx, and they contain no
corrections in Boswell's hand. I judge that they
were corrected by Malone during some illness or
indisposition of Boswell's. It is to be feared that
the joy of seeing his book in proof sometimes led
our Boswell to convivial indulgence in port, which
made the correction of his pages well-nigh impossible. At any rate, signature H (pages 49–56)
shows plain evidence of such incapacity : for he
has made four attempts to alter "the scantiness
of his circumstances" to "Johnson's narrow circumstances," and has barely succeeded on the
fourth attempt.

After November, 1790, Boswell had no further
help from Malone, who was obliged to go to Ireland. A third hand appears in the proof-sheets
when Malone's is no longer found. It may be that
of Mr. Selfe, the "corrector" at the printing-office,
but I do not think so; for Selfe read the proof-
sheets *after* they were returned by the author.
The hand I cannot identify, but it is that of a
learned man.

Some day there will probably be found a copy of the "Life" more interesting than any which is at present known to exist. I refer, of course, to Boswell's own copy. It may perhaps still be in the possession of the representatives of the Boswell family. I do not know. The Boswell family have persistently repulsed all scholars who have had the temerity to apply to them for assistance. But they have already sold Boswell's own copy of the "Tour," which is said to contain annotations by the author on nearly every page. When the author's copy of the "Life," is found, his annotations will enable some future critic of Boswell to complete this history of the composition of that work. Meanwhile, the reader no doubt feels that he has already had enough.

Boswell's Seal or Bookplate

CHAPTER XI

THE MASTER OF AUCHINLECK

I HAVE called this book "Young Boswell" because it seemed to me that the spirit which imbued his entire literary work was essentially youthful. Even in the rôle of hero-worshipper, — a simple conception of him which has satisfied many critics, — there is something of youth and its illusions. When Boswell was at his best, there were present in him the qualities associated with youth, — confidence, buoyancy, hope, and an appetite for experience, — as well as the common faults of youth — self-indulgence and self-esteem. It may seem presumptuous to add, at the end of a book devoted to a study of this youthful spirit, a final chapter on the latter years. They are not a pleasant study. In them Boswell felt the swift retributions of middle age; but he kept until the very end, much of the boy about him. He was always expecting some happy turn of fortune or some revocation of the edict of destiny. As the misfortunes of his middle age crowded upon him, he murmured at his lot; yet there was, had he been able to realise it, a relentless consistency in his sufferings, for they all sprang from an over-indulgence in his peculiar pleasures.

One of these was a passion for London, the like of which Johnson himself averred that he had never seen. Had Boswell been willing to live quietly at Auchinleck during nine months of the year, visiting the metropolis only during "the season," except when he was engaged in putting some literary work through the press, a very different end might have been his. But the old fire raged in his veins. He felt it necessary to transfer his residence to England, to send his sons to Eton and Westminster, respectively, and to educate his daughters in the ways of London society, eradicating every trace of the Edinburgh manner.

The first steps towards this were made possible by the death, in August, 1782, of Lord Auchinleck. Boswell was thereafter free from the restraints imposed upon him by a querulous and dissatisfied father. But he was not happy in his inheritance of the great estates at Auchinleck. He had embarrassed himself by debts, contracted in his father's lifetime, which were now a burden upon the estate and a serious reduction of the income from it. He might perhaps have relieved himself by alienating some of the recently acquired property, had he not taken as much pride as ever in being a member of the landed gentry and in

The Master of Auchinleck

Engraving by E. Finden, from a portrait by Sir Joshua Reynolds

having "a hundred men at his back." It might be desirable to go and live in London with men of genius, but it was imperative, also, to preserve all the lustre of the Master of Auchinleck. Unhappily, the income from the place was not adequate to all the demands upon it. In 1789, Boswell confessed to Temple that, though the rent-roll was above £1,600, the payment of annuities and interest on debts, together with necessary expenses on the estate itself, reduced his income to about £850, and of this, in turn, he had to spend £500 on his five children.

To live in London, moreover, had necessitated something very like a change of profession. When he was well over forty years of age, the fulfilment of his ambition to be an English barrister compelled him to qualify for admission to the English bar, like a youngster in his twenties, by residing a certain number of terms in the Temple and studying the manifold differences between English and Scottish law. These differences are, of course, appalling; and Boswell, at any rate, never mastered them. Although he was called to the English bar in the Hilary term of 1786, and for a time cherished the hope of getting some briefs, — if not in London, on the York circuit, — it took but three years to dispel all his illusions. In 1789, he wrote to Temple: —

I am in a most *illegal* situation; and for *appearance* should have cheap chambers in the Temple, as to which I am still *inquiring;* but in truth I am sadly discouraged by having no practice, nor probable prospect of it. And to confess fairly to you, my friend, I am affraid that were I to be tried, I should be found so deficient in the *forms*, the *quirks and the quiddities* which early habit acquires, that I should expose myself. Yet the delusion of Westminster Hall, of brilliant reputation and splendid fortune as a barrister, still weighs upon my imagination. I must be *seen* in the courts, and must hope for some happy openings in the causes of importance.

All this was most deplorable, because it meant not only a failure to acquire a new profession, but the complete disuse of the old one. When Boswell's father died, the younger man had still a respectable practice, and one which was susceptible of considerable development. But it was all sacrificed to the charms of London.

One of the distressing evidences of human blindness is our inability, not only to appreciate our blessings, but even to know that we have them. Boswell longed all his days for fame, and fame was given to him, in rich measure, and of a kind destined to grow rather than decline with the years. Yet at the very moment that he was known to every reader in England as the author of the "Tour to the Hebrides," he was babbling to Temple about the joys of Westminster. The greatest biographer who ever lived longed, with a juvenile longing, to be James Boswell, M.P.

Of Boswell's unsuccessful attempts to get into Parliament — that is, of his relations with that hateful and unscrupulous politician, Lord Lonsdale — I propose to say nothing. It is a record of boot-licking by Boswell, on which I do not care to dwell. As I make no pretension to writing his biography, I am happily released from the necessity of following him into passages of his life which are neither amusing nor profitable, and which are of no value in revealing the origin or quality of his genius.

But there was one activity of his closing years which has only recently been revealed, and which displays Boswell in a new capacity, with duties which he discharged, so far as one can judge, skilfully and kindly. A number of letters have recently come to light which show us that the Master of Auchinleck was a just and generous landlord. Most of them were addressed to Andrew Gibb, the young factor on the Auchinleck estate, and they were placed in my hands by Mr. James Gibb of Wembley, his great-grandson and last direct descendant. In a letter in which he courteously gave me permission to copy these documents, Mr. James Gibb told me that he had the

papers from his aunt, herself a granddaughter of
the factor, who, however, desired "to remain
anonymous." "She is old-fashioned enough,"
adds Mr. Gibb, "to be rather jealous of the reputation of the biographer, and I think her intention
in voluntarily placing these letters at your disposal
is to show him in the rôle of a landed proprietor
who, by endeavouring to be strict as well as just,
realised his responsibilities to his family and his
tenants."

As the last of Andrew Gibb's daughters lived
until about 1890, it is clear that we have, in this
opinion, a reliable family tradition regarding Boswell during the thirteen years in which he directed
the affairs of Auchinleck.

This tradition is borne out by the evidence in
the letters. Considered merely as letters, they are,
of course, devoid of interest, but they do show
us a man dealing with a work to which he is com-
petent, and, though financially embarrassed, yet
in general just, compassionate, and attentive to
detail.

The following may serve as a specimen : —

LONDON, 4 *June*, 1791.

ANDREW, —
You have done very well as to the cattle and sheep;
and you will remit the proceeds by a bill, that I may dis-
tribute the cash.

The Manor of Auchinleck

Declared, upon somewhat doubtful testimony, to be the work of the Adam brothers

As to Andrew Arnot, he seems to be in woeful circumstances. But I incline to indulge him so far as not to sell his cattel, and in short to try if he can recover.

As to George Paton, I am sorry to see him falling back so. He has a cautioner for five years' rents, and if he does not pay up equally with the rest, I mean his Whitsunday money rent and Candlemas meal, let him be proceeded against; and if he fails to pay, proceed against his cautioner. But do not deal harder with him than with others; I mean, let his Martinmas rent remain unpaid till I come home in August.

Let me add as to Andrew Arnot, that if he suffers his cattle to trespass, and if there be an appearance of much debt to others besides me, his stock and crop should be secured for my behoof.

I think John Lindsay in Skilburn a good man, and therefore accept of his proposal of six pounds for the grass crop, with liberty to dig the yards so far as not in grass. That is, I believe, about his old rent; for he paid one rent to me and the other to the original tenant's widow.

However ill Andrew Dalrymple has behaved, I relent, and you will act in terms of my note at the foot of his letter, which I enclose.

Let Archibald Steel know that I cannot judge of his case till I see his farm. But neither he nor any one else upon my estate has reason to fear that I will be a hard master.

I recollect no more at present, but remain
Your wellwisher,
JAMES BOSWELL.

It is clear that Andrew Gibb was not obliged to be the kind of factor that was known to Robert Burns in the same county a very few years before, and that James Boswell was not the kind of absentee landlord who disgraces the pages of British history. The letters to Andrew are full of human touches and of vivid glimpses of Auchinleck — a fallen tree, the encroachments of the river Lugar, the collapse of "a large part of the old house," dear to Boswell as "an old acquaintance." "I am sorry for David Murdock's heavy losses. Be easy with him. How is my young Muirland pony thriving?"

There is a far-away echo of the French Revolution, which Boswell deems it necessary to put down by any means ready to his hand : —

What does John Stirling mean by apprehending commotions? Bad people attempted to raise them here. But the wise and worthy majority have united so firmly that all fear is over. In case any seditious deceitful writings have been dispersed in our neighbourhood, I send you two copies of Judge Ashurst's "Charge" and "One Pennyworth of Truth," which may be posted up in smithy's and lent about. Paste one of Judge Ashurst's "Charges" in the office, that all the tenants may see it.

On May 31, 1793, he writes the following interesting sentence which, if the purpose expressed in it had been carried out, would have filled his life with new interests and saved him, perhaps, from the dissipation into which he was sinking. "Next month I am going abroad on a tour of Holland and Flanders and to pass some time with the combined armies." His intention, in other words, was to go and visit the Austrian and British allies in their attack upon the towns of Northern France, and to be present at the siege of Valenciennes. If he could have gone, what a volume of reminiscences he would have written! He would have met everybody in the allied camp, and we should have had the pleasure, not only of listening to their conversation, but of reading of all Boswell's emotions *in tempore belli*, while he surveyed the battle from afar.

But in June he was attacked and robbed while he was drunk, his head was cut, and he was knocked about in a very sad fashion, so that he was confined to his bed with pain and fever for many days. He was still determined to go, however, when he wrote to Andrew Gibb on the third of July. Towards the end of that month he paid a visit to his friend Bennet Langton, at Warley, where Langton was a major in the Royal North Lincolnshire militia. But the old enthusiasm was gone; he did not stay out his visit, and candidly owned to his old friend that he had had enough of a camp.

On his return to London he wrote : —

In my convalescent state, another disturbed night would have hurt me much.

O London! London! there let me be; there let me see my friends; there a fair chance is given for pleasing and being pleased. . . .

I hesitate as to Valenciennes, though I should only *survey* a camp there. Yet my curiosity is ardent.

But his recovery was slow, as may be seen from the following letter to Sir Michael le Fleming, Baronet.

LONDON, 31 *July* 1793.

MY DEAR SIR, —

Your kind desire to hear from me flattered me much, and I should sooner have written to you, but could not communicate what I know you would wish to know, my perfect convalescence. I am not yet free from the consequences of the *villainous accident* which *befell* me, being feeble, and not in my right spirits. *Pourtant il va bien.* I met at the Circuit at Chelmsford our friend Bailey Heath, who desired I would present his compliments to you. Indeed, as you love your friends, your friends love you.

London is, I think, emptier at present than I ever saw it. This moment I have had the agreable news that Valenciennes has surrendered. I shall celebrate it today at the Mess of the Life Guards, where I dine *soberly*, as I must do at present. Were you in London, your superexcellent Claret should flow.

The second edition of my "Life of Dr. Johnson" (in which I have paid a just compliment by name to your honour) is come out, and goes off wonderfully. I ever am, with most sincere regard for my dear Sir Michael, Your attached friend and faithful humble servant,

JAMES BOSWELL.

The reader may think what he likes of Boswell's associations with Sir Michael, for nothing is known of them; but it is to be feared that they were not altogether admirable. The superexcellent claret and, no doubt, the superexcellent port that flowed

To James Abercrombie Esq.
of Philadelphia —
from his much obliged
humble servant
The Authour.

Inscription in a Presentation Copy of the second edition of the "Life"

so freely in his house were not calculated to develop the genius of James Boswell. He was courting illness and disaster, for, as he approached the end, he was drunk very often. He was the victim of sorry jests, with which readers of the later and sadder years of his biography are sufficiently familiar. In February, 1795, he tells Andrew Gibb how he had had his pocket picked of a letter and a handkerchief — doubtless when he was in such a condition as to be ignorant of what was going on about him. But the end was now not far distant.

His essential gaiety of disposition never deserted him. About a fortnight before his last illness seized him, he wrote in his usual buoyant way to a new flame, Lady Orkney, a countess in her own right, and nearly two years a widow. She had met him at the estates of her late husband at Taplow, and had, apparently, told him that he was "gallant and gay." He is now desirous of "waiting upon her," for she had promised him mutton at Clifden. "I only say, do not hastily engage yourself. I am your Ladyship's warm admirer."

From his sick bed he dictated a letter to Warren Hastings, congratulating him on his "honourable acquittal," and assuring him that, as soon as he might be able to "go abroad," he would fly to him, "and expand his soul in the purest satisfaction." Of Hastings he had seen something since the beginning of "the magnificent farce," and he was, of course, an ardent sympathiser. In the letter to Hastings Boswell told how his physician, Dr. Warren, gave him the pleasing assurance that his sufferings were nearly at an end. On the "assurances" given to the sick, who shall rely? Our Boswell was indeed nearing the end. He wrote no more letters. He died on the nineteenth of May, three days after the anniversary of his first meeting with Johnson.

During these latter years, his chief literary occupation was the revision of the "Life of Johnson," and the third edition was far advanced towards publication when the author's death occurred. To the reader who knows the many excesses into which he fell, the wonder is that he lived to complete and publish a work of such epic proportions as the "Life." After it was safely "out," he not unnaturally relaxed his ambitions, and was content to bask in the reputation which it made for him. The desire of completing it had pulled him through many fits of hypochondria; but when the task was once done, he had no ambition left for the other books which it had once been his hope to write. That he could not bring himself to undertake them has cost him dear, for it has meant that his reputation has been well-nigh submerged by that of the man whose life he wrote. In various odd ways critics have tried to deprive him of all right to his reputation. I have a friend who once told me that he was engaged in reading the "Life of Johnson," but skipping every reference to Boswell himself — "Boswell without Boswell," as he put it. This, I should suppose, must have been a more dismal experience than reading "Hamlet" without the Prince.

And then there have been "selections" from the great book, — as if part of its greatness did not reside in its very magnitude, — and countless other attempts to conceal the artist who wrought the work and who, with all his merits, certainly never aspired to that of self-obliteration. But at last the tide has turned. The world has wearied of preaching at Boswell, and has consented to enjoy him. But the supremacy of his position would have been clearer, though it could hardly have been surer, if he had completed some of the other works which he had in mind.

The literary projects which he formed from time to time were numerous. He planned an essay in appreciation of Addison's poetry, and a history of King James IV, of Scotland, whom he styles "the patron of my family." He planned a life of Thomas Ruddiman, the classical scholar. We have seen that he intended to publish his reminiscences of Hume, and to do a biography of Sir Alexander Dick. One of his less-known plans was to write a series of stories for children. When he was twenty-three years old, he bought a volume of chap-books, containing the stories of Jack and the Giants, Doctor Faustus, Guy of Warwick, Johnny Armstrong, and others, and wrote the following inscription in it: —

Having, when a boy, been much entertained with Jack the Giant-Killer, I went to the Printing Office in Bow Churchyard and bought this collection. I shall certainly some time or other, write a little Story Book in the style of these. I shall be happy to succeed, for he who pleases children will be remembered by men.[1]

Reference has already been made to his wish, expressed as late as 1791, to recount his travels on the Continent and his conversations with the Great. "I can give an entertaining narrative," he said to Johnson regarding this project, "with many incidents, anecdotes, *jeux d'esprit*, and remarks, so as to make very pleasant reading."

No less interesting was his plan for writing the history of the invasion of Bonny Prince Charlie in '45, which he wished, magniloquently, to call the "History of the Civil War in Great Britain in 1745 and 1746." Once, when he and Johnson were nearing the town of Derby, he observed that they were that day to stop just where the Highland army did in 1745. "It was a noble attempt," said Johnson, who was, sentimentally, as much of a Jacobite as was Boswell himself. "I wish we could have an authentick history of it," said Boswell; to which Johnson replied, "If you were not

[1] Catalogue of Messrs. Sotheby, Wilkinson, and Hodge (Sale of the Auchinleck Collection, 1893), p. 7.

an idle dog, you might write it, by collecting from everybody what they can tell, and putting down your authorities." At that time (1777) Boswell resolved to carry out the suggestion. Four years before, he and Johnson had met Flora Macdonald in the Hebrides, and had heard from her own lips the story of Prince Charles's escape from Scotland, after the disasters in the south. If the account which Boswell records in the "Tour to the Hebrides" is a specimen of the kind of information he could still pick up, it is to be regretted that he did not pursue his original intention; for he would not only have preserved facts which would have been of value to historians, but would have written a book as interesting as a novel of Walter Scott's.

But when all such regrets are recorded, it must be admitted that there is, perhaps, no permanent loss; for such works, had they been written, would but have served to set off the other. They would have been the foil to the "Life." The splendour of that book is in no danger of being forgotten. Perhaps, as the years pass, the chief danger to which it is exposed is that of being talked about rather than read. But it has seemed to me that something might be said in proof of the essential amiability of the man who had the genius to write it — a man, who with all his weaknesses was cheerful and gay, always eager for the punch-bowl to be brought out and the talk to begin; a man who loved drollery more than most, and knew that the sublimest moments in life took on point and lustre by being set over against the actualities of daily existence; a man, too, who, even in his folly, was more natural than most human beings will care to admit.

INDEX

ADAM BROTHERS (JAMES, JOHN, ROBERT, WILLIAM), 8.

Adam, Robert B., 231.

Adam, Robert B., Jr., owner of the only known proof-sheets of the *Life*, 230 *ff*.

Adams, Rev. William, 194, 228, 233.

Addison, Joseph, 252.

"Ameté, Mlle., the Turk." *See* Emetulla.

Appian Way, the, 78, 79.

Arblay, Madame d' (Fanny Burney), her *Diary* quoted, 34, 111, 187, 188, 217; her feeling about the *Life*, 188, 189; mentioned, 149, 227.

Armstrong, Daniel, 80, 81.

Asquith, Herbert H., 214.

Asquith, Margot, 214.

Auchinleck, Lord, B.'s father, advocate and judge, extent of his estates, 7, 8; the Boswellian crest, 8; his relations with B., 20, 21, 96, 97, 98; his views of the purpose of B's visit to Holland, 22, 23; B.'s "management" of, 23 *ff*.; decides to send B. to Utrecht, 30; and Lord Keith, 42, 43; consents to B.'s visit to Germany, 43, and to the Italian tour, 46–48; was good material for B.'s literary purpose, 97, 98; his opinion of B.'s associates, 98; refuses to sanction B.'s addresses to Zélide, 155, 156; effect of his death on B.'s position, 240; mentioned, 29, 30, 37, 127, 138, 139, 141, 150, 154.

Auchinleck estate, 7 *ff*.; the cabinet, and its contents, 89, 90, 192; B.'s debts a burden on, 240, 241; his creditable ·record as Master of, 243 *ff*.

BARBER, FRANCIS, 228.

Barnard, Rev. Thomas, 194.

Beauclerk, Topham, 171, 194.

Belle Irlandaise, La. See Mary Anne.

Benoît, M., *L'Atlantide*, 61, 62.

Berlin, 39, 44, 45.

Berlioz, Hector, 180.

Blair, Kate, "the Princess," B.'s wooing of, 138 *ff*.; hears of B.'s rash talk about her, 145; B.'s rivals for her favour, 146, 150 *ff*.; in Edinburgh, 146, 147; B.'s interview with, detailed by B. in letter to Temple, 147–149; rejects B.'s suit, 152; B. again a suitor to, 159.

Blair, Mrs., 138, 139, 140, 145, 159.

Boswell, Alexander, of Auchinleck. *See* Auchinleck, Lord.

Boswell, David, B.'s brother, letter to, 10.

Boswell, Mrs. Euphemia, B.'s mother, 7 and *n*., 82, 83.

BOSWELL, JAMES, his *Ode to Tragedy*, and its dedication, 1, 3; his ambition to associate with the Great, 3–5, 6, 10, 11, 62, 119; his curious sense of humour, 5; dedication of his *Cub at Newmarket*, 5; his social status, compared with Johnson's, 6; his origins, 7; though heir-apparent to Auchinleck, longs for London, 9; Auchinleck and Ulubræ, 9, 10; first impressions of London, 10; seeks association with literary genius rather than rank and riches, 11, 12; his early life, 11; first meeting with Hume, 11, 12; his judgment of Hume, 12, 13 and *n*.; escapes being a prig, 13; his· disorderly education, 13, 14;

House, 83, 84; brings Wilkes and Johnson together, 85 *ff.*; fails to entice Johnson to Wilkes's house, 86, 87; his later relations with Wilkes, 88, 89; the cabinet at Auchinleck and its treasures, 89, 90, 192; what might have been, 90.

Reason for his preference for the society of older men, 92, 93, 94; familiar conception of, as a hero-worshipper, erroneous, 93; why he teased Johnson about the freedom of the will, 93, 94; always seeking advice, 94, 95; what he gave in return, 95; his attitude defined, 95, 96; his filial affection gradually extinguished, 96, 97; but his imagination fascinated by his father, 97, 98; his love of a good story inherited, 98; his father's opinion of his associates, 98; relations with Sir A. Dick, 98 *ff.*; his Italian tour, 100, 101; his visit to Herculaneum, Naples and Rome described in letter to Dick, 101–103; was his enthusiasm sincere? 103; travels with Lord Mountstuart, 103; proves John Dick's title to baronetcy, 104–106; proposes to "Boswellise" Sir A. Dick, 106–108, 252; relations with Paoli, 108 *ff.*; his sympathy with America, Ireland, and the Scottish Highlands, 109; becomes interested in the Corsicans, 110; his first meeting with Paoli described by both, 110, 111; Sir G. O. Trevelyan quoted on the *Tour to Corsica*, 112; solicits articles on Corsica from friends, 113; publishes *British Essays in Favour of the Brave Corsicans*, 113; H. Walpole quoted on Paoli and, 113; his account of Paoli's reception in England, 114, 115; Paoli's house his headquarters in London,

115; his enduring friendship with Paoli, 115, 116.

Sir W. Temple his constant confidant, 119–121; his dreams of greatness, 120, 121; his conception of a worthy mistress of Auchinleck, 121; his passion for Miss W——t, 121–123; his relations with Mlle. de Zuylen (Zélide), 126–136; his extraordinary letter to her, 128 *ff.*; his "preposterous humour," 132; Zélide decides not to marry him, 135; their correspondence continued, 135, 142, 143; submits her letters to Rousseau, 135; were they suited to each other? 135, 136; the Italian Signora at Siena, 136, 142, 143; the problem of his relations with the sex laid before Paoli, 137; woos Kate Blair, "the Princess," 138 *ff.*; his instructions to Temple on his visit of inspection, 139–141; in the emotional rapids, 142; his intrigue with the "Moffat woman," 144, 145; effect of his other affairs on his relations with Miss Blair, 145; his rivals, 146; describes to Temple an interview with Miss Blair, 147–149, 150; conspires with Fullarton, 151, 152; is finally rejected by Miss Blair, 152, 153; success of his *Account of Corsica*, 153, 154, 157; Zélide proposes to translate it into French, 154; recurs to his idea of marrying her, 154; but is disenchanted, and welcomes his father's refusal to entertain the idea, 155, 156; smitten with *la belle Irlandaise*, 156, 157; writes of her to Temple and Sir A. Dick, 157, 158; has a relapse in favour of Miss Blair, 159; visits Ireland, 159, 160; how to approach the Lord Lieutenant, 160; *la belle Irlandaise* again in the ascendant, 161;

Gibb, James, 243.

Giffardier, Rev. Charles (Mr. Turbulent), 34, 35, 187, 188; letter of B. to, 35.

Gilmour, Sir Alex. ("Sir Sawney"), and Miss Blair, 150, 152, 159.

Glasgow University, B. a student at, 14, 29.

Goldsmith, Oliver, no letter-writer, 173; letter of B. to, on *She Stoops to Conquer*, 173 *ff.*; cancelled reference to, on proof-sheets of *Life*, 232, 233.

Gordon, Hon. Charles, 39.

Gordon, Duchess of. *See* Maxwell, Jenny.

Gray, Thomas, letter of H. Walpole to, 62, 63.

Grenville, George, 66, 67.

Gronovius, Abraham, 30, 38.

HACKMAN, REV. JAMES, 166.

Hague, The, 37, 38.

Hailes, Lord. *See* Dalrymple, Sir David.

Halifax, Lord, 67.

Hamilton, Duchess of, 215.

Hastings, Warren, B.'s last extant letter written to, 250.

Hawkins, Sir John, *Life of Johnson*, 223.

Hector, Edmund, 194, 236.

Herculaneum, 39, 101, 102.

Hervey, Thomas, 194.

Hill, George Birkbeck, his edition of the *Life*, 197 *n.*; *Johnsonian Miscellanies*, 227; mentioned, 231, 236.

Hogarth, William, 64, 90, 91.

Holland, Lord, 112.

Horace, *Epistles*, 9.

Hume, David, B.'s first meeting with, 11, 12; his *History of England* and *Natural History of Religion*, 11; B.'s judgment of, 12, 13 *n.*, confirmed by Mmes. du Deffand and Geoffrin, 13; in B.'s

"ludicrous print," 60, 61; mentioned, 58, 89, 99, 252.

IRELAND, B.'s visit to, 159–161.

Italian Signora, the, 136, 142, 143.

JAMES IV, of Scotland, 7.

Johnson, Samuel, his social status compared with B.'s, 6; quoted, on Auchinleck castle, 8, 9; B.'s relations with, a vindication of his ambition to associate with the great, 14; accompanies B. to Harwich, *en route* to Holland, 31, 32; his advice to B. on places to visit, 39, 40; quoted, on Rousseau and Wilkes, 83; and Wilkes, brought together by B., 85; B. fails to induce him to dine at Wilkes's house, 86, 87, 88; B.'s record of his conversation, 169, 170, 195, 197–201; visits Hebrides with B., 206 *ff.*; B. urges him to write a narrative of the tour, 208–210; his narrative not satisfactory to B., 210; B.'s "Remarks" thereon, 211, 212; his fame as a writer of travels eclipsed by B.'s *Journal* of the tour, published after J.'s death, 213, 214; his friends outraged by B.'s book, 214, 215, 216, 217; his Dictionary, 233; mentioned, 32, 37, 70, 89, 92, 93, 94, 126, 144, 163, 166, 167, 180, 181, 182, 183, 184, 185, 186, 187, 189, 190, 194, 195, 201, 202, 203, 204, 205 and *n.*, 219, 220 *ff.*, 240, 251, 253, 254. And *see Works*, under Boswell, James, for references to the *Life of Johnson*, and *Journal of a Tour to the Hebrides*.

Johnson Club Papers, 231.

Johnston, John, of Grange, a dear friend of B., 19; letter of B. to, 20–22.

KAMES, LORD, 146.

Life, 115; their friendship never broken, 115; his house, **B.**'s headquarters in London, 115; consulted by **B.** as to his relations with the sex, 137; mentioned, 41, 89, 92, 94, 103, 153, 160, 167, 172, 185, 186, 203, 206.
Paoli, Penn., 109.
Parliament, **B.**'s vain attempts to enter, 243.
Paul, Saint, 46.
Pepys, Samuel, his *naïveté* and **B.**'s, 15.
Percy, Thomas, 194, 215, 222, 228.
Perreau brothers, 166.
Pitt, William, Earl Chatham, 42, 160.
Pope, Alexander, 99.
Porter, Lucy, 194.
Porteus, Beilby, 184, 185.
Prestonfield, 98, 99, 100.
Pringle, Sir John, 154.

RAMSAY, ALLAN, 99.
Reynolds, Sir Joshua, 88, 214, 236.
Rivarola, Count, 110.
Rogers, Rev. Samuel, quoted, on the neglect of duty of **B.**'s executors, 193.
Roman Catholics, **B.** associates with, 166.
Romantic Movement, the, **B.** a child of, 181.
Rome, **B.** on the antiquities of, 102; mentioned, 39.
Rousseau, Jean Jacques, his *naïveté* and **B.**'s, 15; **B.**'s method of approach to, 49, 50; his *La Nouvelle Héloïse,* 52, 57; **B.**'s interview with, 53, 54; **B.** asks advice of, concerning music, 54, 55, and tries to "draw" him as to duelling, 55–57; **B.** describes to him his interview with Voltaire, 59, 60; **B.**'s "ludicrous print" increases the ill-feeling between Voltaire and, 60, 61; **B.** submits Zélide's letters to,

134; mentioned, 42, 44, 48, 63, 83, 89, 101, 141, 166, 180.
Rowlandson, Thomas, 215.
Rudd, Mrs. Margaret C., **B.** and, 166, 167.
Ruddiman, Thomas, 252.

SALLY, **B.**'s daughter by the "Moffat woman," 145.
Scotland, Johnson's dislike of, 207, 208.
Scott, Sir Walter, 254.
Scott, Sir William, 225, 226.
Selfe, Mr., corrector of the press, 237.
Seward, Anna, the "Swan of Lichfield," 223, 224, 228.
Shakespeare, William, *Othello,* 146.
Sheridan, Richard B., 171.
Sheridan, Thomas, 1.
Sibbald, Sir Robert, 144.
Smollett, Tobias G., 66.
Sommeldyck, the noble house of, 30.
Southerne, Thomas, *Oroonoco,* 4.
Stewart, Andrew, 37, 38.
Stuart, Charles Edward L. P. C., the "Young Pretender," 65; **B.** plans to write a history of his invasion, 253, 254.
Stuart, James F. E., the "Old Pretender," 44.
Stuart, Col. James, 184.

TAMAR, ballet, 61, 62.
Taylor, Dr. John, 195.
Temple, Rev. William, **B.**'s lifelong friend, 11, 119, 120; sent on a visit of inspection of Miss Blair, with instructions, 139–141; disapproves **B.**'s propensity to intrigue, 141, 142; disapproves of Zélide as a wife for **B.**, 154; one of **B.**'s literary executors, 192, 193; mentioned, 138, 144, 145, 147, 150, 155, 156, 157, 181, 212, 223, 227, 241, 242. And *see Letters,* under Boswell, James.
Thrale, Henry, letter of **B.** to, 208; mentioned, 111.